ISBN 978-1-331-59645-5
PIBN 10210701

ACKNOWLEDGMENT

I WISH to express my sincere gratitude to the Editor of *The School Guardian* for leave to reprint several of the sketches in this book.

PREFACE

THE Public Schools have been for many years now the object of much strange criticism, the greater part of which has run in two main channels: the most readable and undoubtedly the most just being that of the great novelists of our time who, themselves unhappy at school just as they are miserable in the equally imperfect adult world, have given full rein to their spleen in uncontrollable abuse. The other school of critics has been (unwittingly) more damning: it consists of those successful clergymen, dons, and schoolmasters who have never had reason to doubt that all was for the best in the best of all possible worlds: they had no vivid sensibilities nor any tendency to stray from the normal way of the average, unimaginative man of the world; their schooldays were happy; they have been obsessed by no doubts; they thank God that they have no bees in *their* bonnets, and as a thank-offering they write fulsome panegyrics of their own old schools that make the lover of truth and the educational idealist fume with wrath.

Those few, like Mr. G. F. Bradby, who have seen and readily acknowledged that the Public

School system is not altogether satisfactory, and yet are quite sure in their inmost hearts that reformation must come from within and slowly, are only too rare.

We have been told frequently since August 1914 that nothing will be the same after the war as it was before; that "Literature, Art, Music, Politics, Education, all are in the melting-pot; the iconoclast is at work; this is the day of the destroyer; all rebuilding must remain in abeyance for the nonce . . ." and so on.

It is just this point of view that I most vehemently oppose.

We of the Public Schools were working quietly long before the war towards a certain definite goal; we are still, in adverse circumstances, struggling to keep our eyes on that same dim vision, despite the noise of the anarchist; we knew perfectly well that we should vindicate our position in the event of a war; the point at issue is, can we still vindicate our position in the event of a peace? Complete destruction and rebuilding would be the ruin of England: we must proceed on our own lines, gradually eradicating old tendencies which were in danger of vitiating and sapping our vitality.

There is something not merely sentimentally but ineffably precious in the spirit of the Public Schools which once lost could never be regained; it is not merely that all those qualities which make for success in war are educed, but in the more troublous days of peace that are coming there will be a need for just those faculties which seem to be the especial property of men brought up in this peculiar atmosphere. Our faults are known to all: an idolatry of physical prowess to the detriment of the cultivation of the brain, a lack of imagination, and a blindness to the beautiful which almost passes belief. These things, I maintain, can be and are slowly being remedied. Our good qualities are not so easily summed up.

My object in publishing these slight sketches of Public School life before and during the war is solely to bring home, so far as I can, the point that though there are many things wrong with the system, our revolution must be, as we are, typically English: there must be no cataclysm: "Here a little, there a little; precept upon precept, line upon line"—that is the only way by which we shall preserve the continuity of a life that is one of England's greatest assets.

There is some talk at the present time among short-sighted people who can penetrate no farther into the future than next month that Education, after all, matters very little.

It apparently has to be writ large, as I write it now, and repeated often as I do in this book, that nothing matters in comparison with Education.

Our whole object and aim in life is to remodel it nearer to the heart's desire, so that those who come after us may benefit from our work. And those of us who have the modelling, the shaping of the plastic, malleable clay of the children's souls are of all God's emissaries the most responsible. If England fails, it is our fault; if England leads the world, the praise is due in no small measure to us.

For verily every man knows in his heart that it was during his all-important formative years at school that England really helped or hindered the emancipation of his entity, the widening of his outlook, the realisation of his ideals.

S. P. B. MAIS.

January 1916.

CONTENTS

A PUBLIC SCHOOL IN WAR TIME

CHAPTER I

THE BEGINNING OF A WAR TERM

THE news from the seat of war was disquieting; the casualty lists had been for days appalling; our dearest friends, undergraduates of our era, famous in their all-too-brief day for their deeds in the football field, in Parliament, in the world of letters, boys who were in our form but six months ago, all have poured out the "sweet red wine of youth," had given all their hopes of future glory, work, or leisured ease, the serenity of old age, their hope of immortality on earth,—sons that might have been,—and here were we gathered on the platform at Shercombe Magna, too old, too young, or too decrepit to fight, going back to preserve the continuity of Winchborough traditions, stirred by the example of our faithful dead to do our little best to keep England's honour untarnished, her shield of glory bright.

Talk was on one subject alone—the horror of the war, the enormous number of old Winchburians killed in the last four weeks.

We were, perhaps, unduly depressed; there seemed to be no prospect of any finish to this stupendous struggle; there seemed to be no possible ulterior motive of good to be gained from this wanton waste of splendid manhood. We went to bed tired, dejected, nervous of what was to come, unable quite to see how we could keep up the spirit of optimistic endeavour and high ideals among our boys while our own hearts and minds were so obsessed by the black terror of it all.

Sleepless, we tossed and worried through the night till merciful drowsiness overtook us and we were swept into the fairyland of dreams, where life's hideous realities of bloodshed and desecration have no place.

I was awakened by the singing of a million birds—dawn was just breaking over the wooded hills. A glow of heartfelt thankfulness filled my being; jumping out of bed, I hurried to the window and gazed out over the peaceful scene.

All the weariness of last night seemed to have vanished: surely these tiny messengers carolling at heaven's gate could be none other than the liberated souls of my dead friends, whose dust, now mingled with the Flanders soil, would in the future ages cause to spring up a richer race, in whose blood should flow something of that English joyousness of heart, that English laughter, that English endurance, courage, self-sacrifice, and milk of human kindness which have made us for ever famous in the annals of the world's history.

What need for sadness, for retrospective gloom, for dread of things to come?

With a sigh I turned and . . . slept like any "two-years' child."

The sun was pouring into my room when next I woke. A busy day was in store for me.

Assembled in chapel I saw the hundreds of faces I have so grown to love, all fresh with the imperishable glow of youth, all imbued with the God-given gifts of health and determination. We rose, and in a moment the rafters of the old oak beams rang again with the refrain, "New every morning is the love"; prayers were offered up for those "who by sickness or wounds shall be called away to the bosom of God," and we troop out to be welcomed formally as a whole, and informally as individuals, in Big School.

Questions of routine are settled in the masters' meeting; we hear that the Bishop of Southbourne is to preach on Speech Day, but that, "in the light of recent events, all the usual concomitant festivities will, of course, be abandoned"; promotions are arranged; set-lists distributed; and . . . I find myself in form, beginning thus: "It would be impossible for me to begin in any other way than to spend this morning in giving you the life-history and extracts from the glorious achievements of that patriot-poet of whom you have all heard something, and of whose poems I have in the past so constantly read selections to you: I mean, of course, Rupert Brooke, who died on St.

George's Day, on Shakespeare's Day, in the Dardanelles, having offered up, not in vain, all his most precious and rare gifts to the service of that country who bestowed them so lavishly on him. 'What have I done for thee, England, my own?' I will try shortly to show you."

For an hour and more those boys listened rapt to my faltering, poor efforts to reconstruct the life and work of one of our rarest spirits—boys who a year ago might have looked askance on poetry as "all rot" and eyed with suspicion any master who should try to foist on them his own life-passion of poetry. Now they have learnt through tribulation the solace, the uplifting inspiration that comes from that divine outpouring of the soul which we call poetry.

Were nothing else needed to prove the extraordinary, almost unbelievable renaissance that has come about in our public schools since and through the war this hour's lecture on the Shelley of our days and its effect would show the inerasable impression on and the heightened ideals of the boy of 1915.

Now that we may have so short a time to live we no longer can afford to disregard the beauty of cloud and sunset, the budding leaves on the trees, the sheer, exquisite, æsthetic delight wrought in us by the old buildings and cloisters in the school close.

Coming out of school into the hot sunshine of the quadrangle it is almost with a sob of unrealisable joy that we look on the old familiar faces, human yet divine, the age-old latticed windows of the schoolhouse studies, flanked by the flying buttresses of the majestic abbey on either side behind, the elms and yews on the masters' courts, the Tudor gateway, and the beds of myriad-coloured flowers. The scent of sweet-briar sends us in thought back to days of peace spent in shady nooks overhung with lilac and laburnum; we almost smell again the jasmine on the wall; in a moment and we are diving into the sweet, deep pool of "Bunter's Bay," made even more a thing of beauty and a joy for ever by the sight of boyhood, innocent, godlike, frisking on the sides, leaping salmon-like from the pure delight of living, about the cool, pellucid waters.

The summer term once again. Clad in white flannels, ever young, ringing with happy laughter, boys crowd down to nets, and cricket has begun.

Slowly, as if half reluctant to spoil the careless merriment of a single day, come the shades of evening, and the angelus rings in the convent school beyond the fields. Darkness descends, and a stiller beauty, transcending even the glories of the day, takes hold of our hearts; the study windows lighted, the dark forms of boys searching for their books, settling down to work, can be seen. As I go home I pass the many windows of the labourers' cottages, with the lamps flickering on the table or the firelight just casting a transitory gleam on some girl's hair. "Home"! how much more does that word mean now than ever in the past to all of us! My gate clicks, the dogs hear me and, tumbling over one another, come forward eagerly to greet me; this is like old times; term has begun again. In my study, surrounded by my own tattered, precious books, I prepare my work for to-morrow, when we set to work in earnest. How to keep my boys alive to the high service whereto they are called? I know: to-morrow I will give them to learn by heart so that they may treasure it in the "secret'st" recesses of their souls that epitaph I read them to-day. Surely the example of a noble man will go further not only to preserve the sacred spark, but to fan it so that it will become an all-devouring flame of devoted service, than all the teaching in the world.

"If I should die, think only this of me:
That there's some corner of a foreign field
That is for ever England. There shall be
In that rich earth a richer dust concealed:
A dust whom England bore, shaped, made aware,
Gave, once, her flowers to love, her ways to roam,
A body of England's breathing English air,
Washed by the rivers, blest by suns of home.
And think this heart, all evil shed away,
A pulse in the eternal mind, no less
Gives back somewhere the thoughts by England given;
Her sights and sounds; dreams, happy as her day;
And laughter, learnt of friends; and gentleness,
In hearts at peace, under an English heaven."

With lighter heart I close the books and go to bed. With inspirations such as this who could fail to touch the hearts of boys and lead them on to thoughts of highest things, and deeds that will make the name of England ring down the ages as something ineffably precious? After the happy warrior, the schoolmaster of to-day is by far the most to be envied of those who mould and influence the nation of the future. Let us see to it that we fail not at our post; our advantages are indeed great, and so in proportion are our responsibilities. The summer term is here; let us make the most of it; with eyes uplifted and shoulders braced we go forth to meet the unknown. Let it never be said of us in after years that we failed our country just when she needed us most, but rather let us strive so that Englishmen of the ages to come shall look back on us and say, "Here and here did *England* help me: how can I help England?"

This, and this pre-eminentlv, is the spirit that we are born to breed.

CHAPTER II

THE O.T.C.

In the old days the O.T.C. meant one thing only: Camp. All the drudgery of company drills and battalion parades, all the weary afternoons spent in route marches and on the range, were only endured as part of the agony which had to be gone through before we earned the reward of the long-looked-for annual camp at Tidworth, Rugeley, or Aldershot, about which we rhapsodised before and were ecstatic on our return home.

Scarcely any of us except the ultra-keen ever took the corps seriously. For a moment, on looking at our commissions, signed by George R.I. himself, we had an inkling of the meaning of it all; there were, too, some masters who spent their hard-earned holidays training in barracks or attending the autumn manœuvres—but these were looked upon askance as cranks.

The majority of us looked on the corps as "a bally sweat," "piffling waste of time," "playing at soldiers," and so on according as the mood took us. We were rather inclined to grudge the valuable hours when we might have been finishing an all-important house-match to a lecture on extended order or outposts or to a rehearsal of a ceremonial march past.

Frankly speaking, most of us looked upon the day on which the weekly parade took place as the most boring, the most to be dreaded of all; somehow the bath after drill was never quite the exhilarating pick-me-up that it used to be after a really hot game; consequently, we went into school after it slightly depressed, ready to be irritable at trifles, not at all in the humour either to teach or to be taught. The many masters and the few boys not in the corps "groused" because their afternoon was spoilt by the rest of us who were not obtainable for "footer" or cricket. Those of us who had been on parade invariably found food for adverse comment on the manner in which the O.C. had carried out his scheme, or were thoroughly angry because we had been dismissed at least five minutes later than usual.

True enough, we had our lapses into keenness; after a high dignitary from the War Office had lectured us severely on our shortcomings or implored us to join the all-too-insufficient (in numbers) Special Reserve, or just before or after the big Terminal Field Day with Marlborough, Cheltenham, and Rugby, we were full of energy. But more commonly the summit of our ambitions was realised if we could manage to be last on to parade and first off.

Camp, however, made up for it all: it was a holiday with all our dearest friends accessible, sharing it with us; it was a colossal picnic, a throw-back to pre-civilisation days, a time when any kind of food was seized upon as if we were on a desert island, a place where no school bell was for ever ringing us from classroom to classroom, where one rose before the lark and was asleep before it too, where mimic warfare was practised daily as if it were the real thing, where so many Regular soldiers helped us to play the game that we almost felt ourselves to be Regulars too; where in the evening-time we met and "hobnobbed" with all the other public schools of whom we had heard so much, but knew so little, at those never-to-be-forgotten "sing-songs" where camaraderie prevails almost in perfection. One would scarcely dare to say how many of our lifelong friendships have begun, been cemented, and kept flourishing by the Public School Camps.

It was in the midst of one of these great social gatherings that the bomb of war burst. Much time has passed since then. What of the O.T.C. of to-day? It is certainly no stretch of the imagination to say that the corps is the one thing that matters just now at the public schools. At a bound, on the instant, it came into its own.

Every member of Common Room who could went out to fight in the real Army; those who could not have come in to help the Army in the making.

We parade daily instead of weekly, sometimes even twice in the day. There are schools whose members live in khaki both in term-time and the holidays, but these are the exception. With the coming of the holidays, unless we go to train Kitchener's Third Line, we doff our uniforms and appear shamefaced as civilians, some with the gilt-letters O.T.C. in their button-holes, the majority simply in mufti as a relief from the term. For term-time is really strenuous these days: it is not to be supposed that our work has deteriorated, our games been neglected,—rather have they both improved,—it is simply that we have had to find room for this new all-important occupation, that of soldiering.

We do not need compulsory measures to make our boys keen; compulsion would probably act as a deterrent. The corps is as voluntary a society as ever—but everybody belongs to it, to his eternal honour.

In old days any excuse to get off parade was seized, but now the boy who wishes to escape a drill is not to be found; the trouble is rather to keep him back when he has a severe attack of influenza from taking part in night operations when it is snowing, or a biting east wind threatens to penetrate the most military of greatcoats. Everything is now done with precision and finesse; the tactics to be employed on a field scheme are discussed openly throughout the school long before the exercise takes place, and what ought and ought not to have been done for weeks after by even the smaller fry. You may see a house captain taking his team on to the field in a final house match with a sangfroid that you cannot but envy; the next day, perhaps, you will see the same boy, entrusted with a delicate piece of military strategy to work out in practice, absolutely shivering with funk. To such a pass does unbridled enthusiasm bring us.

A new alternative has been introduced for those who are useless at cricket or physically unfit to play football. These now form squads of Morse signallers, and they can be seen on all the high points of vantage in the country surrounding the school valiantly "flag-wagging" from their stations. Semaphore signalling, of course, is learnt by every boy in the school, but Morse makes too great an inroad into our all-too-scanty hours of leisure to be successfully practised throughout the corps.

Distance-judging, scouting, map-reading and map-drawing, bridge-building, miniature-range firing, band practices, extra drills for individual houses—innumerable side-issues of our corps life occupy all the odd half-hours which used to be sacred to detention, swimming, choir practice, "punt-about," and "nets." With all this special training it is not to be wondered at that we treat our weekly battalion drill as an occasion for extra smartness; the least mistake on our part makes us grind our teeth with anger and feel glaring idiots where in the past we should have dismissed the error with a careless laugh. But our greatest efforts are reserved for those splendid occasions when we are included in divisional manœuvres or take part in night operations: these latter in particular stimulating the imagination, for it is hard for the least sensitive of us to fail to feel the eerie influence of the dark. Every bush or tree trunk becomes a real live enemy, every cry of bird or rustle in the trees is only too easily mistaken for the whispering of a hostile force or the creeping of the foe in the undergrowth.

We have learnt more than we ever thought possible of Nature and her ways from these nocturnal expeditions; we have learnt how far noise carries on a windless evening; we have learnt something of the protective colouring of plant and ground to keep our position hidden from the enemy; we have discovered the deceptive properties of water and hillock, valley and green plateau, when we are endeavouring to estimate distances to the nearest ten yards; we have learnt how easy it is for a great number of men to hide themselves from observation within a few yards of those searching for them if only they keep low and preserve absolute silence; to our astonishment we have found, to our cost sometimes, that it is just as possible to ride right over men in furze bushes without dislodging them as it is not to rouse hares or grouse when we are beating for them.

We are learning slowly how to outwit a cordon when we have to break through a line on a moonless night, just as, when it is our turn to form the cordon, we are discovering how to post our men to the best possible advantage so that casual scouts shall not penetrate our outposts. I have seen it urged somewhere that all this sudden renascence of interest in military strategy and tactics is bad for boys; that the outcome of it will be a love of militarism, which is just what we are striving with so great a sacrifice and cost of men and money to eradicate from the world. But from what I have seen as an officer in the O.T.C. my impression is that bloodshed and war are absolutely repugnant to the boy-mind; he is keen, keener than he ever was, to join the Army and to do his bit, but he is no lover of war for its own sake. It is one thing to be an ardent signaller or bugler, and quite another to want to kill a fellow-creature; it is one thing to play a sort of hide-and-seek in the dark on a wintry night in a blizzard, but quite another to want to kill your antagonist if he falls into your hands.

As a preparative for future service in the field the O.T.C. is of vast importance, but if all war were, by the mercy of God, to be abolished to-morrow the O.T.C. would still have its uses for the young citizen who will afterwards control and sway his fellow-men. It cultivates the powers of endurance, it teaches the use of absolute discipline, it generates the ability to command bodies of men, it breeds self-reliance and quick initiative in moments of crisis, it fosters an understanding, and consequently a love of Nature in all her wayward moods and caprices, it keeps boys out of doors in all sorts of weather when they might be mooning about in their houses, it prevents games from being exalted to an unwarrantably high place in the school curriculum, as it also prevents them from being played day in, day out, *ad nauseam*, so that a boy has nothing else to think about—no other interest in life—but the propelling of a ball or the correct attitude or stance to adopt when he goes in to bat; it is a safety-valve for the feelings, an added interest for those who are tired of work or unlucky in the games.

Those who continually praise the public school system for the splendid qualities which it engenders, and admire without stinting the average product which it produces, have been apt in the past to underestimate or neglect altogether the part which the O.T.C. takes in the forming of the altogether praiseworthy characteristics which they hold up to honour. It is to be hoped that future historians will be careful to pay honour where honour is due, and not omit to make mention of the never-sufficiently-to-be-praised Training Corps, which at present is showing to all the world of what stuff public school boys are made, and how the name of Englishman is not likely to be besmirched in one year or two by those who are now about to go out into the world and stand in the limelight of the arena of life—be it political, martial, or philosophical.

CHAPTER III

NIGHT OPERATIONS

WE of the public schools have gone mad over a new craze. In the slack years of peace we fell a victim in the dim ages to diabolo, then a little later to model aeroplane building ; more recently the cult of the motor bicycle ousted flying from its prior place of honour, and conversations ran interminably on " makes " and carburettors, two-strokes, and sparking plugs. The old days of stamp- and egg-collecting gave place to the album of motor number-plates and " bonnet " designs. These in their turn have now been discarded for something definitely military ; after becoming keen on mere ceremonial parades, a colossal effort of the imagination, we have again been bitten with the craze-germ ; this time it is for night operations.

Field days nowadays are sufficiently exciting, but they fade into pale insignificance when compared with any of our tactical exercises in the dark. Our initiation into night work was such an overpowering success that we have been restive ever since.

It was on a bitter night in late November that twenty of the senior N.C.O.'s and men under the C.O. gaily marched away from the town over the desolate moor to tea at a farmhouse unknown to the rest of the school; after their meal they were to attempt to cut through a cordon, drawn by sixty of the remainder of the corps under four officers, stretching over four miles of country. On this occasion I was in defence. At 6.30 I led my fourteen men, singing merrily, through the streets until we reached the darkness of the open country. We then, in silence, broke into the double across the fields in order to get quickly into our position. I said in silence, but the coughing and wheezing, the clinking of buttons and rifles, and the swish of the feet through the grass would, for the first five minutes, have led an enemy to believe that a battalion at least was on the march.

After stumbling over every tussock and grumbling under their breath at the darkness for about four hundred yards, my party gradually became more seasoned to their work, so that by the time they were in a possible danger zone they were creeping by hedgerows with the stealth of polecats. They could even cross the hard, frozen roads on the sides of their soles without a noticeable clatter. Coughs and heavy breathing had marvellously vanished, and it was impossible to distinguish the men's approach farther away than fifteen yards, although they were wearing white hat-bands.

Having placed each patrol on his beat, I did some private scouting alone, first by trying to get into touch with the party on my left, who had unwittingly left a gap between us of three-quarters of a mile, which luckily the enemy did not discover; then I dodged in and out trying to evade the vigilance of my own scouts, every time in vain. I found them holding up carts, bicycles, motors, wandering Yeomanry with their sweethearts, old men, women, and children, for the pure joy of seeing how they jumped.

For two hours in the biting wind and frozen lanes they kept guard, never for a moment relaxing the efforts, frenziedly excited the whole time, imagining "every bush to be a bear" and every rustle in the trees or brushwood to signal the advent of the enemy. But we had no luck; at 9.15 three rockets signalled the conclusion of the experiment, and no one had dared to cross our paths. On the return march news was brought of the capture of three out of the four groups that had tried to force a passage; each of my men was ready to swear that the fourth did not penetrate his beat.

A few days afterwards it was our turn to try to get through the line. Of course, it was a much lighter night; we were certain of that. All the way along on our outward march in the interval of songs you would hear such remarks as "Good gracious! look at the moon; we shall be spotted half a mile away; we haven't an earthly; the Major *would* choose an easy night like this to get his own back . . ." and so on. We thought of all the excuses that could be made for our failure, which we all talked about as inevitable, and yet had privately decided in our own minds that so far as in us lay we at least should not fail.

After a march of some three miles we were halted and given our orders. This time I was on the extreme left in command of eight men, waiting like hounds in leash for leave to begin. When the signal came we dashed off across three open fields to the shelter of a large quarry, from which I had decided to start. Immediately in front lay a dangerous lane extending right across our whole front, which I felt sure the enemy would be guarding. It was pure folly to make for gates or openings, so we crawled through the wet stubble to a place where the hedge seemed to be thin, but where no obvious gap could be discerned, and on a given command made a rush for it, tumbled into the lane, and dived into the undergrowth on the farther side. Here we sustained our first casualty; one of my senior men, in jumping, broke his glasses and strained a muscle, which naturally impeded our progress, but so elated were we at getting past so difficult a place that we forgot all minor troubles, and rested for a moment, panting, but joyful, in the dark red loam of a freshly turned ploughed field. Our scouts went ahead to scour the next hedge, reported all clear, and we crept silently to it; then with another rush, slightly less frenzied than the last, we dropped on the farther side, and anxiously waited for some sign of a roused enemy. All, however, was quiet, so we pursued our course.

This next field was of enormous extent in every direction; by keeping rigidly to the middle we thought that we should escape the snares and attention of any watches on either flank; but when we were half-way across we suddenly dropped flat on our stomachs at the sound of approaching voices. Far away it is true they were; it seemed on a distant road; but it was enough to make us creep on all fours for a hundred yards or more, until at length we were within fifty yards of our next hedge. I then, as scout, crept forward to search for the enemy, and wishing to ascertain where they were before we smashed another hedge, I crept towards a large gap, where I felt certain one at least would be. I was some twenty yards away when a hatless, overcoated creature sauntered casually past the opening with the full glare of the town lights behind him in the distance. In the heat of the moment, so angry was I to think that he should thus expose himself, and at the same time have taken off his hat, which, bound with white, was the sign of hostility, that I quietly remarked, without thinking, "Come along, sonny, put those hands up," to which, when he recovered, he replied, "I'm afraid *you're* dead; I've got my men covering you." "All your men are covered equally well by mine behind me," I retorted. But argument leads nowhere and wastes time. I gave myself up as prisoner, and as a compromise one of my uninjured men was allowed to penetrate this line unmolested. It turned out to be the only line. How bitterly I blamed, as I sat there, my idle curiosity; how safe and near home we should have been had I been content to go on breaking hedges and rushing through.

I was furious at the unfairness of the enemy in removing their white hats, which would have been visible for many hundred yards, and, cold and angry, I begged leave to be allowed to return home. Getting colder and angrier I revolved in my mind over and over again what I should have done; I ought to have given a great shout when I was captured to warn my men to scatter, as I had said in my first instructions; I ought not to have given away the fact that I was accompanied at all; I ought to have crept back silently to my own body and worked out a passage through the hedge as far as possible away from this sentry group; a thousand alternatives flitted across my mind as the town lights became clearer and my way less muddy. I regretted again my folly until I had worked myself up into a sort of minor paroxysm which was only relieved by a humorous accident.

On my way, looking for more of the enemy for amusement to while away the dreary walk home, I heard noises on the farther side of a hedge up which I was creeping; noiselessly I drew nearer, and then to revenge myself for my earlier humiliation I jumped out on them with the remark, "Good gracious! you're the right sort to guard a line of defence; I could hear you a mile away; just try to keep a bit quieter . . . oh, Heavens! Sorry . . . I thought . . ." I had unwittingly surprised a pair of nocturnal lovers, a convalescent soldier and his girl, frightening the lass nearly out of her life, and making even the man forget to swear. That incident did more to repair my lost temper and bring me to my senses than anything. When I arrived at the armoury to report myself I found that I had scarcely a "grouse" left about the wearing of white hats. I was captured, dead, longing for a hot meal, a boiling bath, and a long sleep.

The next day I heard to my delight that all the other groups of our party, except two of mine who came quietly along the high road unmolested, had also been captured by patrols without headgear. Much bitter discussion had arisen therefrom, which was washed out and forgotten the next day in an afternoon attack in the drenching rain on the local Yeomanry, who supplied fresh fuel for the feud incident even to peace campaigns. The desperate stealth of the scouts and screen as they crept through the castle woods, vainly endeavouring to prevent their approach from startling the pheasants, rabbits, and rooks, made them completely forget the ignominy of the night before.

So it is with all our military strategy this term. We no sooner lose our tempers, cry out with shame at defeat, or gloat over victories than the next day we are given a chance to readjust the balance by proving ourselves tacticians where yesterday we had been fools, and fools where last time we had displayed real acuteness. All the time we cannot help feeling thankful that we are learning all this peacefully instead of suffering death or shame after every mistake; we suffer quite enough even playing at it as we do from the jeers of our fellows not to repeat an error, and for that alone, if for no other reason, we are learning an enormous amount that we failed to know before. We are keen; we are beginning to understand that the country is not the open book to us which we thought it to be; we are realising that it is easy enough to understand the regulations and ideas which we read in "Infantry Training," but a very different thing to put them into practice; that the half has not been told us of the intricacies or the charms of night work; that, instead of a meagre chapter of instructions, there ought to be a special volume devoted to what has become with us, as I said at the beginning of this chapter, a passion and a craze.

CHAPTER IV

A FIELD DAY

NOTHING could be more different from the spirit shown towards a field day in November 1913 than that which animates the schoolboy of to-day.

Then the whole show was looked upon as a colossal "rag," a heaven-sent opportunity to get away from routine and have a real slack time; no one cared in the least as to the objective or the point of the scheme—that was a business for the officers to settle amongst themselves; they were equally unconcerned whether a grim umpire announced that they had been heavily defeated or had won a sweeping victory. All they thought of during his discourse was tea.

But nowadays when a tactical scheme is suggested for a certain day you will see the O.T.C. board besieged hourly by myriads of keen soldiers-in-embryo anxious to learn what the fate of their platoon is to be. "I hope to Heaven that we're not in reserve"; "Have you heard that Malchester, Cliffborough, Upton, and Harbury are all to be on our side?" "Sloppy told me yesterday that all the ground we're fighting over is inches deep in water"; "Yes, and there are three great streams, ten feet across and three deep, with no bridges . . ." and so on.

Rumour runs rife as to the number of rounds of blank that is likely to be issued ; lights may be seen late at night in various classrooms where keen N.C.O.'s have obtained their form-master's permission to "jelly-graph" contour maps for their sections ; shops are crowded the night before these great days with boys securing provender to supplement the rations which they suspect will be insufficient.

At last the morning of the fight comes. Fags, who have no trade union to protect them, are "hoicked" out of bed as soon as it is light to put a final polish on their seniors' buttons, to fill the water-bottles, to clean the puttees and boots. Somehow it takes about three times as long as usual to dress on these occasions, and a frantic haste only results in just scrambling on to parade when the O.C. has reached a critical point in his long detailed description of the day's programme.

At last, after a decalogue of "dont's" with regard to the throwing of personnel from the carriage windows, we march off to the station amid a fanfare of trumpets, cheers from the townspeople on their way to business, and counter-cheers from the errand-boys and school-children on their way to school.

We line up on the platform, the special glides slowly in, the bugle sounds the "Entrain," and helter-skelter the whole six hundred make for the corner seats immediately facing them. Broken windows are avoided by a miracle; the train starts: immediately volley on volley of wild raucous cheering on the part of the corps re-echoes through the station and the woods behind, and we are on our way to the rendezvous.

The officers snatch a glance at the news and take their only chance of a pipe until evening comes; all too soon the train draws up at a siding and the bugle rings out the permission to detrain, and we are again in a twinkling all lined up ready for our long march to the battlefield.

Tongues are loosened, sections of fours wax more friendly than they are wont to be in the constraint of school, and talk of a really intimate nature ensues until the talkers find themselves deafened by the noise of music-hall ditties and hymns whistled, sung, and played on divers instruments all round them.

For a few moments they bawl at the tops of their voices, only to continue their conversation in a lull as if there had been no break.

Some few, oblivious of the beauty of the lanes through which they are passing, of the discordant yells on every side of them, placidly read on in their favourite book,—*The Thirty-Nine Steps*, or Edgar Allen Poe, for instance,—lost to all sense of the present, rhythmically but unconsciously keeping step.

After some five miles of this, the column is halted, made to pile arms, and allowed to fall out for an hour. Some continue to read, some settle down to a game of chess, others go to sleep ; one crowd goes off to rob an orchard in a body, and returns with haversacks, pockets, pouches, and hats crammed to overflowing with cider apples, which they proceed to devour apace before questions are asked.

A distant tramping is heard, and suddenly interest is revived—here comes Malchester, one of our great allies, swinging down the road.

Every one is thinking the same thing : "How much bigger and smarter these fellows look than we do !" We fear and admire them. That they are probably thinking much the same about us does not cross our minds.

Lunch rations are then served out, and silence reigns while well-nigh a thousand boys attempt each of them to cope with two great hunks of ham sandwiched between four vast layers of bread, one banana, and two Bath buns.

Scarcely are the last remnants out of sight than we start to discover the enemy.

We are in wooded enclosed country, but by aid of the maps we think that we know our way. It is only after an hour's ploughing over wet grass and stubble that we find that we have been facing due south for three miles when we were trying to go west.

Curses are launched against the officer in charge of the advanced guard, and the column changes direction at last after having delayed the action for the best part of the morning.

By devious routes, through hedge and brier, through farmyards the scent of which cries aloud to the heavens, through orchards laden with apples green and apples red, apples yellow and apples brown, the companies wind their way; at length the noise of firing on our left shows that our left flank guard have got into touch with the enemy's scouts. The column is halted and the preordained dispositions are made. No. 1 platoon goes south to seize Marshbarn Farm and make good the only foot bridge across the river of which we have heard so much, No. 2 platoon hurries still farther south to try to get round the enemy's right flank, Harbury takes the main road to the north, and the remainder of us (the main column) remain in our breaches until such time as scouts bring back news that our way is clear to make a main attack upon some particularly weak spot.

It is hard indeed to remain sitting in the side of a hedge, consoled only by blackberries and apples, while all the luckier platoons are firing heavily with rifles and "rattles" (machine-guns) within four hundred yards.

One subaltern privately dispatches a scout imploring the commander of No. 2 platoon to send back an urgent message for help: he sees no chance of being in at the death otherwise. But it is not to be.

The Harbury leader sends back a note to the effect that he is clearing the road and that it is a good one.

The Major immediately decides to convey his whole force this way and force a passage into the village which it is his aim to destroy. He selects the young subaltern to take his platoon in front. This officer is not slow to avail himself of the opportunity to leave the reserve. He dashes down the road at breakneck speed, makes good the bridge over the river, and feels his way for the high stone bridge over the railway which commands the village. In his anxiety to get some fighting he invents a bogus message to the effect that the bridge must be rushed at all costs, and, taking advantage of a passing train, hustles his platoon up on to the bridge only to find that his "point," cowed by the sight of a platoon of the enemy immediately in front of them, sink on to the asphalt and open fire. In vain he implores his men to come on they stop and open fire . . . an umpire drops out of heaven and caustically tells him that his men are for ten minutes annihilated; that, had he gone on and rushed the enemy he would have allowed him the bridge, but that as he stopped the victory rested with the other side. Deeply chagrined, the subaltern turns his men about and retreats. Meeting a friend of his in command of the next platoon some two hundred yards back, he advises him to rush the bridge while the enemy are thinking over their victory. In a few seconds he hears a mighty cheer and has the doubtful satisfaction of seeing his friend do what he failed to do, and clear the bridge.

His ten minutes having elapsed, he returns to the bridge to find that the enemy have taken up a strong position behind a hedge, holding the village some three hundred yards ahead. Not again is he going to hesitate. Section by section he gets his men into the field and amasses by degrees about five hundred others; these he sends up by half-platoon rushes ten yards at a time, nearer and ever nearer to the hedge; his blood boiling within him, the cries of the opposing commander, "Give it 'em, lads; shove it into 'em now, boys," only makes him the more bloody-minded.

At last he has got to within thirty yards of them, and with one blast of his whistle leads the whole force in one great overwhelming charge. Breaking through the hedge he lands fair and square on the shoulders of one of his opponents, and for five seconds a hand-to-hand fight ensues. Suddenly the umpire again turns up from nowhere and calls out the subaltern, and this time awards him the victory at the cost, as he says, of great loss of life. Five minutes' respite is to be allowed while the enemy retreat. The subaltern goes through each platoon and finds a man missing here, a rifle there, a hat somewhere, a bayonet somewhere else: he rests his men while these are searched for and wipes his overheated brow.

His force is now well in the village and the road is blocked with sight-seers and photographers. The bugle to "Continue" sounds, and for the last time he leads his men away up the narrow village street. A peep through the dense laurels on his left gives him a glimpse of the Hall park, where he detects the enemy opening out in extended order to their final position. He details his friend's platoon to open up a frontal attack while he tries to enfilade them on their left flank: the corner of the market-place is held by the enemy: once more he urges his platoon to a mighty effort, and literally gallops at their head to seize this position: the enemy, taken unprepared, hold on a second too late: he dashes into the middle of them and takes a whole platoon captive, and then opens fire on the remainder, whose left flank is now unprotected. Almost immediately the "Cease fire" goes, and he lies in the middle of the road absolutely exhausted, well content that he has retrieved his honour

Two yokels standing near him exchange impressions:

"Ay, it were fine to watch them lads; 'twer' joost like one of them cinema pieters." "That wer' reel faightin', that wer', watchin' 'em break through them laurel bushes and knockin' of each other down like. Eh! A wish oor Jim 'd bin 'ere to a' seed 'em: 'e allus laiked fist work did oor Jim. Such little lads too. By Goom, to zee 'em run with their guns out like that there; it wer' a fair treat, that's wot it wer'."

Now the various companies begin to assemble from all parts of the park to hear the "pow-pow." Singing in the far distance betrays the fact that some platoons are still on the way to join us. At length all are gathered. The leaders of each side concisely, map in hand, declaim their dispositions, and the umpire starts his harangue.

He is the Adjutant of the Third Castershires, invalided home and doing his level best to maintain the high traditions of his regiment by bringing into it all those public schoolboy cadets whom he picks out on these field days as promising.

To-day he is as caustic in his adverse judgments, as sparing in his praises, as you would have a first-rate and keen officer to be.

He retells the story of the taking of the bridge, for instructional purposes; he causes a thrill of joy to run through the veins of the Winchborough contingent when he says that he had rarely seen a prettier piece of work than their attack across the field and in the village; he begs those who are soon to be leaving to consider the claims which his regiment has upon them; and, thanking them in the name of the country for the work which the O.T.C. were doing, he ceases as abruptly as he began.

Every boy seemed to hang upon every word: even when he dilated on the work of the platoons which were outside the main action, one having to fight a rearguard action all the way home owing to a mistaken direction, he kept the interest of the entire mass awake: for the truth is that in these days boys want to know; they are only too anxious to learn whatever can be learnt under peace conditions.

Amid the cheers of the villagers every one then marches off to the tea rendezvous and thence to the station, which again re-echoes to the cheers of the various schools seeing each other off.

Arrived once more at home, with band playing the "Carmen" we swing up the busy streets and into the lime-tree courts of the school. A word from the O.C.:

"I can remember no better field day. Winchborough is certainly not ashamed of her present generation. Food and baths await you: I will keep you no longer. Dismiss."

. . .

The next morning, in Common Room, the O.C. speaks:

"I hear about half the corps have written to the umpire to ask him to reserve for them a commission in his regiment. In our amateur way I suppose after all we do some good. We don't get much of the honour and glory, but I suppose this is our proper sphere. I wish I was always as certain of that as I am to-day."

CHAPTER V

CHAPEL

ONE of the greatest troubles that besets the mind of the conscientious schoolmaster is the incessant questioning of his inner being as to whether he is doing his utmost for the future welfare of the youth of the nation. Would he not have a stronger hold over boys if he became ordained? Would not the definite doctrinal standpoint that is the *sine qua non* of the man who takes Holy Orders be of the greatest use to him in tackling the many serious but secret problems of public school life?

Every young man has, I take it, had qualms at one time or another about this. I know no more perplexing subject among the many intricate worries that form part of our daily life.

The first and fundamental object of the clergyman is to preach the Gospel, to throw light upon the essential features of the Christian religion, and to bring home as forcibly as he can the necessity of it in every boy's mind. If England is to continue to be the great nation she has become she must be definitely Christian in her outlook; if her youth neglect the tenets of the doctrines held by this religion then the decay of the country is imminent.

But there immediately crowd upon the mind myriad upsetting theories. Am I the type of man to confine myself within the narrow bounds of the Thirty-Nine Articles? Can I justifiably don the garb of the minister? Do I feel that absolute call to preach without which no man can claim inspiration or the right to preach? The pulpit is not merely a platform from which I may "spout" my ideals: it is the place from which I am to interpret and comment on God's Word. My whole life is spent in propagating a sort of gospel: in my classroom, on the playing-fields, everywhere I stand as an example. My influence is paramount: am I not already exerting it to the greatest advantage? What further could I do if I underwent a course at a theological college and finally vowed to spread the accepted dogma as a parson?

Chapel as it now exists is unsatisfactory. At some schools form-masters have to take a sort of roll-call during the service; they have to tick off the names of those present during hymn or prayer, psalm or sermon.

If they are absent they have to arrange for a deputy to act for them. This rankles in the hearts of not a few, who look on a chapel service as a time set apart for public worship and private devotion.

They notice with deep apprehension the listlessness on the part of the boys in the presence of the uplifting words of collects and lessons, the bored somnolence during sermons, and the lack of appreciation during the recital of noble psalms or emotional hymns. Such a state of things at all costs, they feel, should cease to be.

Only one remedy presents itself to them, and that a drastic one. Why not make chapel-going voluntary?

Again and again we hear from parents and old boys the same story: "Oh! I never go to church now; I got 'fed up' with it at school: to have to attend fifteen services a week whether I would or not put me off for ever afterwards."

It seems to me that a general revival of real worship would follow on a scheme which provided for voluntary attendance in chapel. Suppose it were ordained that every boy must attend at least three services a week. I think that the result of such a scheme would very soon tell on the tone of a school. It would do away with the stereotyped routine of the present-day system, and absence now and again would only make the service the more precious to the boy-mind.

Think of the difference in attitude of boys towards the weekly voluntary Service of Intercession in regard to the war on Friday nights and their attitude to the ordinary morning and evening compulsory prayers.

One is a real act of devotion, where the atmosphere is tense with emotion, the others a succession of lifeless lip-services, of little use except to a rare few, and to them only on rare occasions.

As a matter of fact, since the war began the question has been less pressing than before, because nowadays the sonorous war collects and majestic martial hymns of G. K. Chesterton and Rudyard Kipling have done much to bring home to boys the need for prayer and praise, and have riveted their attention by their very strangeness just at those points in the service when their thoughts were most liable to go off at a tangent to house matches or punishments, friends or bathing. But most of all do I think that the new influence is being felt on Sunday evenings at sermon-time. Then do we feel most ready to hear words of comfort or advice from those carefully chosen strangers who come down to uplift and sustain us in our time of trouble and pour out of their fulness words of wisdom which help us to live for another week at the extraordinarily high tension which has characterised us now for nearly a year.

Bishops, dons, headmasters, missionaries, and famous old boys now appear with much greater frequency than of yore, and each has some fresh light to shed upon the attitude which we should adopt at a time when our very souls are being harrowed, our outlook on the meaning of life and the relative values of actualities changing with every day.

It is imagined by so many people that none of our internal difficulties still beset us because the nation is at war. This is not true. We have not only all our old faults to be eradicated, all our old horrors to combat, but the added load of this terrible war to bear; we need all the help we can get. Houses still run amok; individual boys still give way to secret vices; expulsion is not entirely done away even yet; the old appeals to us to fight the good fight, to be straight, to shun evil and to choose the good are as necessary as ever. They need saying, perhaps now more than ever, for much of the evil that went on in public schools was directly due to the fact that boys were in a state of ennui. They turned to the excitement and glitter of vice out of sheer relief from the monotony of the ordinary routine. Now that each boy is chafing, as he never chafed before, to be up and doing, to be away fighting or doing something tangibly, obviously useful for his country, he feels the restraint and discipline of school life to be more irksome than ever, and as a consequence is more than ever tempted to seek for relief in whatever way occurs to him.

In High Church schools, such as those of the Woodard Foundation, it is quite conceivable that he may find such relief in the definite part allotted to him in the services, as acolyte, bearer of the cross, and so on, but in our more normal schools there is no active part given to a boy unless it be the lesson-reading by prefects. I should like to see a state of things brought into being where nearly all those senior boys who wished it might be permitted and encouraged to serve at the Holy Communion or to take some definite part of the service; perhaps some of the apathy is at present due to the sound of accustomed voices taking the services day in, day out, interminably. Out of a staff of twenty or thirty it is rare to find more than three or four men in orders, and the variation in the prayer-reading must perforce be slight; it is, I know, only a point of detail, but it has its direct influence on the attitude of the school towards chapel.

Again, too, I can recollect occasions when a headmaster has had frequently to urge the school to join in the responses, the psalms, and hymns. Particularly is this the case in schools where the choir is very carefully trained and has a reputation to keep up. Surely the foremost principle of school services should be that each boy should join in as often as possible in every part of the service where the congregation is expected to take its part.

Nothing is more touching than to hear an assembled crowd of boys really sing with full-throated vehemence and sincerity a favourite hymn or psalm, which brings me to a most important problem in the conduct of services. The choosing of suitable hymns is one of great difficulty—a strange tune, an unknown hymn does more to damp the ardour of really spiritually-minded boys than anything I know. A few psalms constantly sung, a small list of well-known hymns, seem to me to be the most suitable in existing conditions. There is, I know, the danger lest these become meaningless if the changes are rung on a very small number; to strike the happy mean between the few and the many is one of the hardest of a headmaster's or choirmaster's minor difficulties.

My last point is one of immense importance and overshadows all the rest. At present there seems to be far too great a cleavage between chapel and the rest of our lives. I would, for instance, have the psalms and hymns brought more continually into the ordinary work of the classroom. How splendid an opportunity is offered in the teaching of English from the noble Elizabethan prose as written in the Bible! To divorce the Bible from other books seems to me to be a mistake. It is one of our national characteristics to keep several watertight compartments in our souls: religion in one, chemistry in another, games in another. Until these are all correlated I can see no hope for progress or for a national reformation in our attitude to religion, work, games, or life. Chapel is one of the most formative of the many influences that work on the boy-mind, but if chapel is only one phase of our religion—the most real, I grant, but still only a phase—there is little chance of our turning out the God-fearing, clean-minded, upright citizens whom it is our job, as schoolmasters and guardians of the race, to educe.

CHAPTER VI

HYMNS

"It has been the frequent lamentation of good men that verse has been too little applied to the purposes of worship, and many attempts have been made to animate devotion by pious poetry; that they have very seldom attained their end is sufficiently known, and it may not be improper to inquire why they have miscarried."

DR. JOHNSON, *Life of Waller.*

THE importance of this subject at the present day is apt to be overlooked. Chapel is taken so much as a matter of course, like meals, that it is frequently forgotten that more verse of a devotional type than of all secular kinds is put before the normal, imitative boy. Twice a day on weekdays and at three services on Sundays throughout the term, the boy's mind is confronted by the poetic efforts of our hymn composers—confronted in a way that he finds difficult to disregard; for the fact that they are put to music, and therefore assimilated slowly, naturally tends to every line, every word being carefully thought out and commented on by any fairly intellectual member of a congregation.

It is obvious, then, that the evils of doggerel will be magnified just as the good will accrue from the slow rendering of a great poem. We are privileged to hear English prose at its noblest and most majestic in the Collects and Bible; in the Psalms we are uplifted by the gorgeous beauty of the poetic thought, and by the time that we reach the hymn our minds are malleable, impressionable, attuned to higher things and the most godlike aims. The Spirit of God has descended like a dove, and we are prepared to give up our souls to His service, our lives for His Name.

The hymn is that which "makes or mars us quite." If it happens to be one of the few in the language that combine great literary merit with devotion, the service becomes an ecstasy, a pæan of thanksgiving—æsthetically, emotionally, soulfully we lose ourselves in heaven above; but if the heights to which we rise on the one hand are supreme, to how black a depth do we fall if our senses are jarred, our minds upset, our intellects outraged by some disgraceful rhyming utterance of a mind neither in the true sense religious nor intellectual.

No one is quicker to detect a false sentiment, a hollow ring in speech or in the written tongue than the average schoolboy; once he detects that some of his school hymn-writers are impostors, possessing neither genius, a knowledge of or love for God, nor understanding of the rest of the world, he feels it to be a personal affront that he should be compelled to sing or to listen to these hollow efforts.

It seems to me so important a matter only to

have the hymns of genius that I would only include some of the works of Charles Wesley, William Cowper, Smart, one old Irish hymn that appeared in *The Nation* about three years ago, Ben Jonson, a few of Milton's and Addison's, most of the fifteenth- and sixteenth-century writers, even up to the end of the seventeenth century (including some of the works of Tate and Brady), Newman, Isaac Watts, Toplady, Ken, Keble, Lyte, Milman, Heber, and Williams.

There are very few hymns outside the works of these men that will satisfy that inner craving to be at once uplifted in body, soul, and mind.

To add to our confusion, the words that we are so used to in the Ancient and Modern version have in many cases been wantonly disregarded and others (naturally in most cases worse) substituted—it is a moot question whether any man has a right wilfully to alter the words of a poem; it is a sacrilege if it is real poetry. The hymn ought not to be included if it is not; at any rate we were better off when we had the Ancient and Modern version pure and undefiled—we could at least pick and choose, and if we chose a hymn of genius we could be sure that we were using the author's own words, not a garbled, distorted version to meet the particular narrow taste of a bigoted section of the Church. But having chosen to eliminate and to reconstruct, as the authors of most public school hymn-books have done, the least they could do was to abolish in their select edition such lines as ·

> "Whatever, Lord, we lend to Thee,
> Repaid a thousandfold will be:
> Then gladly will we give to thee,
> Who givest all,"

which if believed and acted on, would inculcate a spirit at once so devilish and commercial (in its worst sense) as to prevent effectually any further understanding of the very elements of Christianity.

To take an entirely different standpoint :—Who that has been brought up on such a passage of real feeling and beauty as

> "He shall feed me in a green pasture, and lead me forth beside the waters of comfort"

can help a thrill of shame and horror when he finds the signature of Addison to the following paraphrase?—

> "When in the sultry glebe I faint,
> Or on the thirsty mountain pant,
> To fertile vales and dewy meads
> My weary wandering steps He leads:
> Where peaceful rivers, soft and slow,
> Amid the verdant landscape flow."

Not only is the æsthetic sense outraged, but we feel towards Addison as we do towards some country parson, illiterate and uninspired, who for a sermon decides "to put into simpler language and explain the story of the Prodigal Son." It is criminal.

But Addison is not content with paraphrase; he must needs amplify; his pen runs riot; he has not the reticence of the Psalmist; he proceeds:

> "Though in a bare and rugged way,
> Through devious lonely wilds I stray,
> His bounty shall my pains beguile:
> The barren wilderness shall smile
> With sudden green and herbage crowned,
> And streams shall murmur all around."

What warrant for this appalling versified nonsense is to be found in the Twenty-third Psalm? In singing a hymn such as this, if we are not entirely asleep, moods, like shivering fits, eddy to and fro through our frame; in this verse disgust and horror give way to laughter. We ask ourselves, what is "sudden green"? But the worst is still to come. We have been taught from our childhood and implicitly have relied on that most inspiring verse of hope and faith:

> "Yea, though I walk through the valley of the shadow of death, I will fear no evil, for Thou art with me: Thy rod and Thy staff comfort me."

There is a good deal of the Bunyan in each of us. That verse, together with the whole of that wonderful Psalm in which occur the words, "Thou shalt not be afraid for any terror by night . . . a thousand shall fall beside thee, and ten thousand at thy right hand, but it shall not come nigh thee," upheld me as a boy during the plague of small-pox at Gloucester and at school when really serious diseases were common—selfishness, boyishness, I grant, but at least they made a real impression on me. The spirit of them at least I do understand now; but what of this translation of Addison:

> "Though in the paths of death I tread,
> With gloomy horrors overspread,
> . . . .
> Thy friendly crook shall give me aid,
> And guide me through the dreadful shade"?

I should like to meet the man or boy who was comforted, elevated, or consoled by that verse, or any portion of that hymn.

I have dwelt at some length on this particular piece of verse, because I feel that if a really sound man, or literary genius, of the stamp of Addison fails in devotional poetry there is something to be said for the Johnsonian theory that contemplative piety, or the intercourse between God and the human soul, cannot be poetical. And yet it was the same man who wrote:

> "Through all eternity to Thee,
> A joyful song I'll raise:
> For O! eternity's too short
> To utter all Thy praise."

Johnson's theory would deny the title of poetry to the hymn which opens:

> "God moves in a mysterious way,
> His wonders to perform;
> He plants His footsteps in the sea
> And rides upon the storm."

It is by a peculiarly Sophoclean irony (so dear

to the heart of Shakespeare and all great dramatists) that at the very time when Johnson was saying that—

> "Man, admitted to implore the mercy of his Creator, and plead the merits of his Redeemer, is already in a higher state than poetry can confer,"

Cowper was writing hymns to prove the fallacy of the statement. Dr. Johnson unfortunately, like many of his followers, had read too much of the "metrical devotions" of Tate and Brady to understand the real meaning of the word poetry.

To substitute "poetry" for "prayer" in the well-known hymn of Montgomery, Johnson would never have recognised that poetry

> "   is the soul's sincere desire,
> Uttered or unexpressed,
> The motion of a hidden fire
> That trembles in the breast."

But quite apart from the true poetic value, there is another side very different but quite as important. We are taught by one hymn to give largely that we may receive more; in some we are taught as good Christians to revel in the tortures of those who have not conformed to our tenets or moral laws.

> "But sinners filled with guilty fears,
> Behold His wrath prevailing:
> For they shall rise, and find their tears
> And sighs are unavailing;
> The day of grace is past and gone;
> Trembling they stand before the Throne,
> All unprepared to meet Him."

And again :

"Every eye shall now behold Him,
Robed in dreadful majesty;
Those who set at nought and sold Him,
Pierced, and nailed Him to the tree,
Deeply wailing,
Shall the true Messiah see."

The side of the friendliness of God, of the outstretched hand, the sympathetic side of His nature, is all too little emphasised ; remember the extraordinary capacity and need for love that a boy has—and think of the effect of such a hymn as

"O Jesus, I have promised
To serve Thee to the end;
Be Thou for ever near me,
My Master and my Friend,"

on a boy of imagination, lonely in the deepest recesses of his heart. This hymn carries with it the reality of religion, the sense of worship, the use of Christ, and it is only when such a mood has been reached that the true meaning of the following verse strikes right home, the heavenly affection strengthening human love:

"And then for those our dearest and our best,
By this prevailing presence we appeal;
O fold them closer to Thy mercy's breast,
O do Thine utmost for their soul's true weal;
From tainting mischief keep them white and clear,
And crown Thy gifts with strength to persevere."

This could only be uttered by a confiding friend to another, more powerful than himself, one to whom he could always turn with entire trust.

What we wish for is less of the

> "Make haste, O man, to live,
> Thy time is almost o'er"

sort of devotion, and more of the panegyric—

> "Human tears and human laughter,
> And the depth of human love."

Less of the

> "Weary of earth and laden with my sin,"

And more of

> "For the thrill, the leap, the gladness
> Of our pulses flowing free."

More of

> "Run the straight race through God's good grace";

More of

> "Chasing far the gloom and terror";

Less of

> "By Thy deep expiring groan."

In a school chapel above everything we want realities ; something to show us that Christianity is an optimistic, buoyant, cheerful, absolutely happy religion where human feelings and failings, successes and misadventures, loves and hatreds are taken into account.

The Bible does so: let us see to it in our wise choice of hymns that they do not fall behind or contradict the truth and splendid martial vigour of the rest of the literary part of our daily services.

CHAPTER VII

SUNDAY

When I was a boy I remember that I looked forward to nothing so much as the weekly walk on Sunday afternoon with my dearest friend.

Then it was that, ambling idly along a bank with a revolver, taking pot-shots at water-rats, lazing in a coppice, pipe in mouth, or sitting in the kitchen of a farmhouse bargaining for apples, we used to get to grips with a world not ours in the hurry and bustle of school life.

We would argue on matters ethereal, on the body politic or civic, but rarely or never thought at all of those petty scandals and rows that encompassed us about in dormitory or in the classroom, on the " footer " grounds or in the tuck-shop, on parade or in the " gym."

We became, as we walked through the invigorating air, citizens of a larger, nobler, more important world, free to let loose our thoughts, constrained and groove-ridden in the precincts of the school and buildings ; we were free to indulge what fancies we would, free to people our finer world with finer companions than we met in hall or sat next to in chapel ; masters and prefects were forgotten, and heroes of make-believe and romance took their place.

As I meet the youngsters of to-day climbing the hill out of the town on Winchborough Downs, or looking for eggs in Lord Poltimore's preserves, I sometimes wistfully gaze into their eyes and wonder if they have the same thoughts that I had when I was a boy,—thoughts that were reluctant to include the prying usher or elder boy, thoughts far away from the world of grind and games: it is on such occasions that I am irresistibly led to ask lonely pedestrians to tea, even when they are not members of my form, set, platoon, or game.

I nearly always repent. They invariably accept, and accept with alacrity; but outspoken and natural as they appear as they wriggle along by my side down into the town, they become tongue-tied and nervous within doors in the presence of my wife, and during tea do nothing but eat as if they were about to die of starvation. They have no small-talk except on the dangerous topics of other boys or other masters; they are willing to recapitulate and go into details with regard to the scandal of the hour, but of the outside world they are ludicrously silent, and feign an ignorance we know to be unreal.

They will discuss revues, musical comedies, and the latest plays generally, varied occasionally by the shortcomings of politicians; but they fight shy at once of topics of real and lasting interest, however tactfully these are introduced.

They are not the same boys we know and grow to love so well in form; all at once they seem to have become gauche, grotesque, out of place.

This must be the reason why the majority of men invite the same boys over and over again and neglect the great majority . . . for once you have made a close friend of a boy you will certainly realise, and probably for the first time, what Bacon meant when he said that true friends halve sorrows and double joys.

I suppose no letters are more treasured than those natural outpourings of youth's desire which come from the heart of a well-loved boy friend; no moments in one's life could be more precious than those all too short minutes on Sunday evenings when the boy escapes to your room, and, lying on the carpet, gazes into the fire and almost as it were in a trance unburdens his mind of all the troubles that beset it, emptying himself to you as to a real friend, asking for help in the sure knowledge that in you he will get it. It is then only that you realise the unfathomable depths, the innate innocence, the awful purity, the clear-eyed vision, of the child-mind.

We are apt to forget our own childhood, to read into the minds of the boys with whom we associate something of our own soiled and tainted ideas.

In the mass no collection of beings is highly sensitive, at all innocent, or (except in rare cases) even pleasant; some strange, malign influence seems to get to work as soon as two or three are gathered together for whatever object. We see boys most frequently in the mass; consequently we are apt to judge them in the mass; but take an individual boy, take him seriously to your heart, endeavour to study his every idiosyncrasy, and you will soon discover, not blinded by love to his vices, but rather through love with your eyes for the first time opened, what a kingdom of heaven in little dwells in the heart of the average boy.

"Rarely the time and the place and the loved one all together."

Sunday is the only day, Sunday the hardest worked day of all at a public school, Sunday full of its chapel-services, practices, rehearsals, literary societies, debates, arrears of correspondence and corrections to be worked off, the very day when we pine most of all for a rest. Let them all go . . . Sunday is the only day when you really get a chance of seeing into the boy-mind, which after all is your life-mission if you are a serious schoolmaster and not merely a "drifter." Sunday is the day when the workaday world can most easily be doffed or forgotten by the boy, when under the influence of sacred things he can most easily show you his natural self, when the craving for human companionship and sympathy overcomes the artificial inbred tendency never to reveal his likes or dislikes to any other human being.

There is a kind of glamour cast over Sunday: we get up later; there is a chance at last for quiet thought ; it comes as a break and relief after six days' monotonous grind wherein all tendency to think is ousted for lack of time.

Shapes of trees and buildings, scenic colours, passing clouds, the mysteries of hedgerows and upland downs appeal to us no more in vain on Sunday, for the luckier among us make time to go and loll about on stiles or by the river-bank and by quiet contemplation regain our lost soul.

By the time that Sunday evening comes round even the dullest of us are ready to be influenced by the preacher in the school chapel ; the warmth, the lights, the sense of nearness to and companionship with our dearest friends all unite to make us more than ever open to impressions. Then, if ever, are we ready to respond to whatever call is made upon our honour ; self-sacrifice and the cultivation of all the higher virtues appeal to us then as at no other time in the week. I suppose there is no other time when a conscientious, keen master would give his whole soul to know what goes on in the minds of boys than on those occasions, when he watches the school file slowly out of evening chapel after hearing the mighty inspiring message of a great preacher who has held his audience spellbound for thirty-five minutes.

Yearningly he turns as he separates himself from the groups of friends and seeks his classroom to prepare his work for Monday morning.

Gradually the hum of voices dies away, the lights one by one disappear, the gates clang to all is silent save for the scratching of his pen . . .

an hour passes. He fumbles his way downstairs to his bicycle, is let out by the school porter and is once more in the garish streets, thronged with soldiers, shop-assistants, Salvation Army bands, motorists, and servant girls. . . . Sunday for him is over. The inspiration dies. Monday and the workaday world lie too near at hand.

But he has had his day, and the halo will not entirely disappear.

CHAPTER VIII

SOME SOCIETIES

At the outset I should like to make clear my fundamental point with regard to this paper. Though I may in the course of it rather poke fun at some school societies which strike me as being typical, it is not that I fail to recognise their worth. What we want is not fewer, but many, many more of them—house debating and dramatic clubs, form reading societies cliques and sets all over the school intent upon improving their histrionic and public-speaking faculties, ready to read papers and listen to others on subjects of literary, political, historical, or philosophical importance. At Oxford it seemed to me that most of the so-called literary clubs to which I belonged were merely an excuse for a revel and an orgie: at any rate they made for camaraderie and a cheerful bonhomie, which was so much to the good; but at school the pendulum swings to the other side, and we find societies like the "Quidnuncs" flourishing on stilted convention like a green bay tree.

The "Quidnuncs" was founded twenty-five years ago by a keen literary housemaster, who collected half a dozen of the most brilliant boys and cajoled them to come to his drawing-room on Sunday evenings after chapel, for the purpose of reading papers and discussing them.

He met with overt hostility from all the rest of the staff, the majority of whom proclaimed their conviction that one term would see the decease of the society. After twenty-five years, without a break of any kind, the " Quidnuncs " still meet Sunday after Sunday.

Modifications, of course, have taken place, changes from the original scheme. It is now *the* literary society of the school; only fifteen boys are allowed to be members, and these are elected by the committee; there are eight honorary members, three of whom are famous literary lights in England, old bovs, who seldom remember to come back; the remaining five are present masters on the staff. Besides these, however, wives of all the married members of the community and several townspeople are allowed to come to these meetings and listen to the papers read.

The young enthusiastic master, full of literary ideals, hangs on the verge of this highly select society, and hungers for the day when he may be invited to join the ranks. He pictures in his mind a scene pregnant with literary ideals: frenzied debates as to the merits of this or that genius, people clamouring to read papers on the merits of their own particular gods, ready to take up arms against a sea of criticism in defence of them. One day he receives his formal invitation.

At 8.15 p.m. he presents himself, palpitating, at the front door of one of the housemasters (the venue now changes weekly from one housemaster's drawing-room to another), is ushered into a room full of people, all of whom are obviously in a state of constraint and strange nervousness.

The subject for this evening is "George Meredith" . . . "a gorgeous subject," thinks our young enthusiast to himself.

Whispers, a shuffling of feet, a dive for a chair, and another breathless silence.

The President speaks. "We are all ready, Hankey."

The reader of the paper, be-spectacled, nervous, white-faced, adjusts his glasses, clears his throat, rustles his manuscript, and begins : "Ladies and gentlemen, after the very brilliant paper read to us last week by Mr. Tarrant-Hinton I cannot do aught but apologise for my halting phrases and the even poorer (if possible) enunciation with which I deliver this paper. . . ."

They all start like that without exception. Our young enthusiast, not knowing this, shivers with apprehension and glances round, to find that no one else has even winced; apparently this is a gambit of conventional openings.

Follows a life of Meredith, bald as a billiard ball and not half so interesting, a patchwork of irrelevant quotations, not a tithe of which does the reader himself even pretend to understand, the plot of *The Egoist* outlined in detail, and, to finish with, a general criticism culled from a paper—and the hour is over.

In the sixty minutes' reading there has not been one original remark, one comment of the reader himself . . . he belongs to a conventional society, he must feed the conventional mind on what it expects, thinks it understands, and can assimilate.

Our young visitor, full of ardour, now boiling over with wrath, unthinking, breaks the silence that follows the hushed clapping of hands that closes each day's paper with, "Do you really think Meredith ever thought that about women; after his own experience, too? You remember that passage in his *Letters* . . ."

"Supper is ready, I think, Harold," interrupts the hostess loudly. The company rises.

Discussion is over: there is no discussion. Conversation at the prolonged agony called supper, which, however, the boy-element seems to appreciate more than the paper, runs on the sermon, yesterday's games, a change in the school rules, and a coming bazaar.

Meredith is not so much as named from beginning to end. Our young man finds this a normal evening. Once, perhaps twice, in the year a young rebel manages to gain access to the society, and is invited to read: he chooses Byron; he says what he means; the club stirs uneasily in its chairs during the reading, honesty frightens it out of its wits; awful, constrained mutterings over the supper-table follow. "The young brute ought to be expelled! The consummate indecency and insolence of it all. How dare he read like that and say such things . . . ? " He is not invited to read again; the society again settles down to its humdrum existence. And yet, even at its lowest stage, the "Quidnuncs" is a club we would not see done away. It does lead boys to read; it does bring before their minds names which its members otherwise would not have heard. But how much would we not give to see it develop entirely as a literary society, where members totally forgot their normal status and responsibilities, and only met to further the cause of literary endeavour, fearless of their fellows, honest and original in their convictions, ready to convince and be convinced.

The " Stolidi " is composed of a very different collection of boys. It is a large society, which may be joined by all boys who have emerged from the Lower School.

It meets weekly in the Big School, and is largely attended, in spite of the fact that the work which ought to be done then has to be made up for out of hours.

Hundreds of boys of varying ages may be seen Saturday by Saturday rushing across the Green Quadrangle with cushions under their arms, and laden with deck-chairs, fighting to get the best places nearest to the hot-water pipes. This is not a " master-ridden " club. The President is a young, earnest man, who thinks that public speaking is one of the most educative influences in a school, and so encourages every type of boy to speak. With this one exception masters do not patronise the "Stolidi," except on special occasions, when two well-known senior men agree to lead and oppose a debate on a subject of which each of them is a connoisseur.

Some two or three plays are read terminally—Shakespeare seldom, Sheridan and Wilde often, the very moderns on rare occasions. It is truly hard to find plays which both touch boys' interests and yet do not come under the ban of the school censor, who is a real martinet.

The Twelve-Pound Look and *The Younger Generation* have, for instance, recently been prohibited, and *Magic* was lucky to escape. The club's greatest successes have been of late *The Rivals* and *Cæsar and Cleopatra*, but such plays are not common.

The evening starts with public business, always an occasion for much heart-to-heart speaking. Local feuds are started, enlarged, and finished here more frequently than even the unimaginative President imagines.

The convention-ridden atmosphere of the public schools is nowhere more evident than on the "Stolidi."

All the old arguments about tradition, the glory of athletics, caste, and custom receive the same salvoes of tumultuous applause; whereas Liberal opinions, iconoclastic ideas, need for reform in any department, always call down hisses or are received in stony silence.[1]

[1] This is no longer true: the Christmas term of 1915 changed all that.

Yet, in spite of all this, there are boys who would never have dared to rouse themselves out of the ruck of nonentities into which they would almost unwittingly have subsided had it not been for the "Stolidi." They have felt themselves impelled to speak on some subject very near to their heart; and once having spoken, the fever quickly gets a grip on them and they rapidly become fluent, reasoned speakers, astonishing themselves and their friends by the ease with which they speak and the excellence of their matter.

If schools are hedged in on every side by custom and tradition, there is perhaps less reverence for either here on the "Stolidi" than elsewhere; but, as in the case of the "Quidnuncs," we could wish with all our hearts that members could forget entirely their prestige and position and speak for once from their hearts, unconscious of self.

Perhaps the most useful club of all which we possess is the "W.N."—"the Wednesday-nighters"—who assemble in Tighe-Warner's rooms (Tighe-Warner is English master of the Lower School), in order to listen while he reads, or tells them famous stories, or declaims passages from well-known plays. This master's sitting-room is capacious and warm; all the Lower boys are made cordially welcome, and lie about all over the floor chewing chocolates and fruit, which the crafty usher dispenses in order to entice them into his den.

The room is lined with well-filled bookshelves,

and each member of the "W.N." is at liberty to remove any book which appeals to him for three days at a time, merely by writing the name of the book he requires and his initials in a large ever-open notebook, which is fastened on one of the window-sills.

Sometimes, when reading palls, each member contributes a short story or poem of his own; and so generous have the contributions of the "W.N.'s" been that there are now three volumes of their works extant.

Nearly all of the work that can with truth be called good is by one boy, but it is a tribute to Tighe-Warner that he should have produced one genius among his tribe; the best part of the rest of the verses and essays is the obvious delight that went to the making of them; artistry and, in some degree, achievement can be detected in even the worst of them. Terminally the "W.N.'s" give a series of half-hour plays to an audience of particular friends; admittance by invitation only, each member being permitted to invite two outsiders. The dresses for these plays come from London; the school custos is bribed to become programme-dispenser, lime-light-man, and scene-shifter; an hilarious supper is given by Tighe-Warner to the cast afterwards; and the next few days he spends in ruefully going over the inroads made by these orgies into his already too slender income. But he knows at heart that it is worth it.

Anything is worth while: the lavish expenditure of much-needed money, the giving up of precious hours of leisure, the despondent moments consequent upon the failure to impress upon one's material one's faith in a particular author—anything is worth while.

More real education is to be found in these literary, dramatic, and social clubs than in any other department of school life ; they develop the gifts of self-expression, of elocution, of the imagination ; they provide the boy with food for thought, with matter that will take him right out of himself and enlarge his ideas beyond the narrow scope of school ; he begins to realise that there is a world elsewhere into which he may expect—nay, will be expected—to enter and probably control.

He learns to exercise his sympathetic faculties, to look with other men's eyes on human life and human suffering. Books he will find are perhaps, as some one has said, a mighty bad substitute for life, but he will also find out that they are at least a very good guide as to how life should be lived. They are, at times, the only source of comfort upon which a man can fall back ; at moments of grave crisis, in ecstatic moments of great happiness a man will retire to his study and turn over the pages of some much-bethumbed, much-loved book, and gain comfort and inspiration therefrom when he needs it most.

But this love of literature must be cultivated when the heart is young and the character malleable. In no better way can such a love be matured than in these clubs which already exist. I would have them, with all their faults, multiplied a million-fold. There would be, there are, there have been, appalling irretrievable mistakes, made with regard to such school societies, but I would risk all that for the sake of the success of the majority of them. Boys are born actors; let them act, encourage them at all times to act; boys have a far finer imagination than most adults; encourage them to cultivate their imaginations by reading and talking about the finest works of genius.

We have been too long in the shadows of the tyranny of the ugly: let us cast off our false shame and openly pursue the beautiful. These literary societies open up the way; let us not let such opportunities slide, for on them depends the welfare of the future of the race.

CHAPTER IX

CRIBBING

THE question of "cribbing" raises two points of quite considerable importance in the educational world: what sort of attitude towards his work does a boy adopt who must needs cheat at it? and what sort of teachers are those under whose eyes such a distortion of true learning can take place?

I am not for the moment concerned with the moral code involved in "cribbing." The whole school code of honour requires drastic handling · nothing less than a revolution will accomplish any realisation on the part of youth that its point of view is all wrong.

Imagine an enlightened age looking on impurity tolerantly, on cribbing as a harmless way of evading punishment cultivated by all who find that it pays, on coming to its masters for sympathy and advice when in trouble as an unforgivable crime, on "cutting" a game as an offence which puts the delinquent beyond the pale of respectable humanity.

I am concerned with its causes and results alone. Whence does this horrible fungus which undermines the whole of school life spring?

Well, partly from parents and uncles. Who does not recollect some such conversation as this from the jovial elder, especially after a good dinner, when all men indiscreetly indulge in reminiscences of their own early life?

"We have heard the chimes at midnight, Master Shallow." "Ha! ha! I remember when I was at Winchborough in old Troddles' form, how we used to pin our 'cribs' on the back of the fellow in front and read the *Alcestis* straight off. He was as blind as a bat. I was in his form for two years and never did a stroke."

"Good Lord, man! why, that's nothing. At Upton, in the Rooster's days, when he used to tell us to shut our books and write the 'props' out there would be a great slamming of books and then the old man would go to roost, close his eyes, and in a minute was asleep. But every one, of course, furtively opened his Euclid at once when he had gone off, and wrote for dear life. I recollect once old Hal Gurney—yes, your godfather, George—old Hal was in an awful stew because when he opened his book he found that he had torn out the pages the term before to crib in exams. with, you know. . . He didn't know what to do—so he started to look over the chap next to him, and suddenly the Rooster woke up and yelled, 'What are you doing, Gurney?' and Hal was in such a funk that before he knew what he'd done he'd blurted out, 'P-please, sir, the pages are out of my book, sir, so I was just looking over Dixon's. Lord!

you should have been there. The Rooster was a regular devil with the cane, too!"

Every one has to listen to stories like this, true or not true (I hope I have not invented two too ridiculous examples; I could so easily have quoted from fact), when schooldays are mentioned over the dinner-table.

In such a way do our major influences condone the offence.

Is it a wonder that a boy straight from a preparatory school (however good), where he has imbibed the strictest ideas on right conduct, finds that the way of life is a wondrous maze when he has endured a month at a public school? He notices that quite estimable people "crib"; he remembers those scraps of conversation at home where his elders took "cribbing" as an essential factor of school life. What wonder that he soon falls into line with the majority! It is the only way by which in some forms he can maintain his position in the class. But I begin to think from my foregoing remarks that my point of view is perhaps liable to misconstruction.

In my own mind I believe that in reality far less "cribbing" goes on than is generally supposed, for several reasons. First, when is a boy in such a position that he must needs indulge in it? I take it that the most common instance is that in which he has not had time to prepare his work for a master who is lavish with his penal rewards in case of failure.

Now, the average man who is a stern and terrorising despot is not of the kind to be hoodwinked by the "cribber." The way of the wicked in this case is very hard; he will find it exceedingly difficult to catch the demon off his guard; an unwary disciplinarian is an anomaly, a contradiction in terms. With a weak man who never dares to punish it is unlikely that a boy will take the trouble to "crib" unless he is exceedingly anxious to score high marks.

But it is futile to indulge in generalities like this; let me take my own case. It is quite on the cards that I am entirely wrong with regard to the impression that I think I produce on boys, but this is how I see myself. In English I take my own form, all of whom are candidates for outside examinations such as the London Matriculation or the Army Entrance. They are united in one aim, that is, to pass as quickly as possible. Consequently I am relieved from the necessity of marking their work at all; what I am there for is to teach, to correct their mistakes, to get them through, and, far the most important in my eyes, to instil a love of our literature into their minds while I have them with me.

There is no question of "cribbing": it would be a pointless pursuit. There is never occasion for punishment, because each of these boys is always doing his best. There is a great deal of extra work to be done, papers to be revised and done again when they fail, but this is not punishment. It is not that I am a stern disciplinarian —far from it. I love my subject; I love my boys; if I fail to interest them or to make them work for the work's sake I have failed. I have no penal code to fall back on.

On the other hand, I take a vast amount of mathematics all over the school. I encourage all my boys to correct the greater part of their ordinary work for themselves in addition to looking over it privately myself. Mr. Jolliffe, who once inspected us, strongly opposed this system on the ground that it bred dishonesty and was a strong incentive to cheating. I am the more inclined to think that I am right and he is wrong when I recollect that the schoolmaster probably knows more of boys than the don who visits them for one week every five years. But I do quite see that it is possible for a boy to give up wrong marks (which after all is only another kind of "cribbing") in this way, and for me not to discover it every time. As I walk round and round the class all the time that boys are writing I like to think that there is never any likelihood of any boy being tempted to "crib." I am not quite sure how he could.

In problems (my most frequent work, of course) he most decidedly could not; in geometry he would find it mighty hard, for (like most modern young pedagogues) I do not resort to the trick of letting boys write out propositions. What "cribbing" there is must go on in the classical forms or where history notes are expected to be learnt.

And this brings me back to general principles. "Cribbing" is just as much an offence against the rights of man as cheating, lying, impurity, or stealing. How, then, to deal with it? First, I suggest, by making work so interesting that boys will begin to work for work's sake. It is no use laughing at such a notion as crack-brained, weak-kneed, or even as an impossible ideal. It can be done, because it has been done. In English I do it, and Heaven knows I am no born teacher. Make a boy see that there is something vastly entertaining in the subject, explain to him thoroughly the use that it will be to him hereafter; if it is a merely disciplinary subject no good in itself, scrap it; scrap it at once and substitute a live subject in its place; the theory that a thing is good for you in proportion as it is distasteful has gone for ever; make a boy see that the subject is your own life-hobby and is every bit as important as (say) cricket or football, that even grown men in the world outside continue such a study for pure pleasure until their lives' end, and the artificial stimulus of marks and examinations—the bane of the usher's existence—will disappear for ever, and naturally with the marks will likewise vanish "cribbing," for there will be no point in it.

Punishment must go; marks must go; and then, and then only, will interest revive and "cribbing" die. It is no use telling me that masters are not capable of bringing this about. Sack all those who confess their inefficiency, and bring in a new *régime*.

It only needs courage, an indomitable optimism, and catching your boy young; it might perhaps be as well to hang all parents and relatives who indulge in dangerous reminiscences, but, as we have neglected parents for so long, perhaps we might continue to do so with impunity. After all, they do not matter much either way ; it is the future we are trying to save, not the past.

Next I would suggest, more drastic even than the first, that not only the Sixth Form, but all the school should be encouraged to use real translations for all their classics. By " real " I mean Gilbert Murray, Jowett, Jebb, and so on, as opposed to Mr. Kelly and all his nefarious crew. By that means there might be a spark of hope that the boy of the future might realise, however dimly, that there really *was* a " grandeur that was Greece " and a " glory that was Rome." Not one in a hundred does under existing conditions. In other words, abolish " cribbing," by making it compulsory.

I do not want to end on a note of pessimism, but I see that I said I would make a remark on the *results* of " cribbing." I should have thought that they were sufficiently obvious ; but perhaps not. Well, in my opinion, a lasting distaste for work is one of the most important. How could you expect a boy to be interested in translating word for word from a Latin or Greek author into a language which is certainly not English, or any other that ever sane man talked, about as intelligible to the average boy as the classics were to Milton's unfortunate daughters ? Remember how they hated their father; affection between a boy and his master is not likely to be fostered if this mischievous system is to be allowed, nay, encouraged, to continue as it is to-day.

The whole point of modern education is to find the bent of a boy's mind and to develop that at all costs in order that when the time comes he may become a specialist in his own line. Cribbing, to make an almost Elizabethan-like pun, simply cabins, cribs, and confines the mind, and prevents it ever expanding on the right lines. Further, I am in agreement with the moralists when they assert that one vice leads to another—a boy who becomes loose enough to crib is well on the way to become loose in all the other departments of life.

Lastly, as well as severing the link which might bring master and boy together in a most desirable communion, it goes even farther, and threatens to sever close-knit friendships between boy and boy, whose codes of conduct will diverge according as one consents to the cribbing mania and the other has the sense to refuse to have his future spoilt even to appease a companion or to hoodwink a master who is scarcely worth deceiving.

CHAPTER X

RAGGING

Ragging consists of two major sorts: ragging of masters by boys (ragging of masters by masters is a delightful pastime, and much more common than the general public would suppose, but it need not detain us here), and ragging of boys by boys (ragging of boys by masters is also a delightful pastime, but of no importance). These two sorts have also two subdivisions—ragging which is healthy and ragging which is unhealthy.

To take the ragging of masters by boys first, if you are not already too confused by my somewhat poor attempt to parody Burton to want to read any more.

I cannot recollect any case in which I think this to have been healthy; but then, of course, I am a master.

The first essential of any man who wishes to become a schoolmaster is that he should be able to keep order; not that he does keep order; the very best masters I have ever known have been those who cultivated a most easy-going manner in form, who really talk and are talked to as if the whole class were on a very successful walking tour or were camping out together. But that he should be able at any given instant to restore absolute silence, to make the form do what he wishes, is of the very life-blood of the successful master.

If a man cannot do this,—it isn't a question of being easy to acquire; you either do it naturally or you never do it at all,—if you cannot do this, go away at once and keep hens, write novels, starve in Bloomsbury, become a fisherman or a miner, do anything that will help you to save your soul alive, but do not stay to be harried and bullied to death by a crowd of merciless little gnats who despise you for not killing them, and whom you despise for their utter inhumanity and savagery. There is nothing more pitiable in school life than the crushed man, the man who knows that all his colleagues laugh at him for being so ineffectual, who goes into form sweating with apprehension, dreading every footstep of approaching "boy," wondering what devilish device the wretches have got in store for him to-day.

Remember, please, that boys have no imagination. Consequently they never tire of being cruel: they are precisely on the same moral level with snakes and cats in this, that their absolute lack of any imaginative faculty makes them smack their lips over the sight of an old man in pain at their malicious efforts to drive him out of his mind again and again and again. They never tire.

Nervous young graduates come to us full of

the theory of education, fully prepared to open their hearts to the innocent young under their control; and they discover at once that until they can show "these innocent young" that behind the silky tongue there lies physical power, they are simply not listened to. I should not care to have to count up the number of absolutely excellent men whom I have known who have come to the public schools fully determined to carry into practice ideals that we simply must bring into being unless we are to go under altogether,—men who have had to leave after one term simply because they had not this gift of being able to make a boy sit down when he had decided to stand up, or *vice versa*.

On the other hand (I am not certain which is the more tragic), how many countless men have I known who are rapidly making names for themselves as successful schoolmasters who under any sane system of education would have been sacked after their first day; men who have this wonderful gift of being able to keep boys in order, but beyond it nothing, nothing at all—they would fail even as policemen; they have no powers of direction; they can only hold their hands up and keep the traffic at bay. Successful schoolmasters indeed! at a time when we are crying out for men of liberal ideas and courage and imagination to come and save us.

But I am supposed to be talking about ragging, a subject on which I am somewhat of an authority, for I spent the best years of my life as a boy in trying to devise new tortures for a man who had been kindness itself to me, but who had the misfortune to stammer and blush. As a consequence I learnt nothing, and he gained a whole-hearted loathing for the whole race of boys.

This ragging of incapable masters by boys is only comparable to the silly goose-cackle of the country yokel when he sees a bicycle "skid" in the wet, and a girl fall and cover herself with mud.

That is his notion of humour; a boy's sense of humour is about as much developed: to see a master or a friend in real agonies (spiritual, of course; physical bullying is slowly becoming unfashionable; we have now got to the refined stage of inflicting torture on the soul: mere arm-twisting was humane by comparison)—this is a source of inexhaustible delight: it is surely a sign of human progress that by the time he reaches Oxford he is content to derive amusement by leaping on to a bonfire made from his own and his friends' furniture.

I can think of nothing in school life which so sickens me as this distorted sense of humour on the part of nearly all boys. One moment and I am passionately declaiming a passage of Shakespeare, making myself believe that I really am cultivating a sense of honour, of pathos, of proportion, of real humour in the minds of my boys; they really look as if they are gaining something; they think they are too: five minutes later they have left me and I hear them in an adjoining classroom shouting, clamouring, unanimous in one great burst of raucous, empty laughter as the blackboard (by special arrangement) falls on old "Flatfoot's" head. It makes one at times almost despair of the whole race of boys; whereas, in my calmer moments, I can quite see that it is not the fault of the boys: it is the whole pernicious system that encourages them to grow up like this. There is no trace of a healthy side in the ragging of masters by boys.

When we come to the ragging of boys by boys we are faced by an entirely different proposition. There is no question that there are some boys who are only saved by being laughed at.

Anstruther, to take an example, comes from a famous private school at Broadstairs: he has been captain of cricket and football, and head of the school; rather too full of his own importance, he comes on to us. For the first month of his new life he is persistently bullied by all the Middle School fags to whom he has foolishly boasted of his pristine greatness. There is no doubt that this "squashing" does him all the good in the world.

Roberts, on the other hand, is a long, lanky scholar, who has outgrown his strength; he is very clever, very keen on his work, but quite useless at games.

He finds himself all unconsciously at first the butt of his house, of his form, and in the end of the whole school: he never has the sense to go for any of even the smaller fry who attack him, owing to his kind-heartedness. Consequently life is made more and more miserable for him; he goes off by himself for lonely walks, and does his best to avoid all society; he begins to think how loathsome all human beings are—in such a way are suicides, cynics, and atheists made.

His whole school life is one long, horrible nightmare; his masters smile when they meet him, and perhaps get as far as thinking "poor fellow": if they go farther and try to make advances, Roberts will retire into his shell at once, and be brusque, and even violently rude from very nervousness.

The worst of it is that there are many boys of about sixteen or seventeen who are just beginning to put on airs, and likely to make fools of themselves, who would be saved by laughter· but no one, as a matter of fact, dare worry them. The Seniors simply don't notice them; the Juniors live in daily terror of them.

These become the young "bloods-about-town," interested only in sartorial effect, unhealthy in mind and body, simply because they have nobody to "rag" them out of their affectation.

A master occasionally takes it upon himself to try to knock the nonsense out of such boys' heads, but the average man is much too apt to confuse cheap sarcasm (most loathed of boys) with humorous ragging. His intervention only serves to make matters worse, and the boys go out of their way to dress so as to upset this master's susceptibilities and render themselves conspicuous.

As soon as it becomes generally known that these expressions of peculiarity are only meant to cause irritation, and not as a species of originality, the entire school endeavours to copy the young heroes, or to do all in their power to help in the scheme for the suppression of sarcasm on the part of masters.

After all, "ragging" is a harmless amusement in nearly every case; the whole subject depends entirely on the possession or lack of a sense of humour in "ragger" and "ragged."

There are some men who will never be cured of silly foibles until they are ducked in a pond; of these are those foolish Bohemians, who think that Bohemianism consists in wearing a red tie and no collar, plush waistcoats and lurid hats . . .; who dispense with forms of custom, courtesy, and manners, to show how superior they are to the world about them.

At school such people are intolerable, and have to be made to conform to the recognised standard by whatever means public opinion can most effectively bring to bear on them.

Boycotting is an inhuman crime; gentle "ragging" is a mercy thinly disguised, and if deftly carried out, may prove to be the turning-point of a boy's life.

Most growing youths need some outlet for their stored-up, little-used vitality, and a useful safety-valve lies here. On the other hand, no people are so consistently cold-blooded, or more unintelligently, unwittingly cruel than a crowd of boys, and it is little short of marvellous that some hunted, unpopular boy is not occasionally driven to suicide by the systematic bullying to which he is treated.

It is when "ragging," which is in essence gentle, degenerates into cruelty, which is in its essence rough, whether intellectual or physical, that a stop has to be put at all costs to the least sign of ill-treatment on the part of any clique of a school.

CHAPTER XI

PREFECTS

It has been said by more than one expert that the crowning glory of the public school system is the ingrained sense of being able to rule that differentiates the public school boy from every other type.

The characteristic ease with which a young, inexperienced Englishman of twenty-three controls a country twice the size of his own is, and always has been, a matter of envy and astonishment to foreigners of all other lands.

"Give a boy as much chance to develop his own initiative as possible"—so runs the tradition; and ever since the days of Doctor Arnold boys have been allowed more and more scope to learn how to govern while they are still at school, in order that, in after years, they may find the reins of government as easy as fielding in a house match or drilling a platoon in the O.T.C.

It is all a question of custom. The only question is—Who are the boys who deserve the honour of prefectorial privileges? Who are the boys most likely to use their privileges aright, and who are those most liable to abuse them?

Roughly speaking, the two types of boys who strive for recognition most strenuously are the Intellectual and the Athletic.

In some schools it is customary for the entire Sixth Form to become *ex-officio* prefects, which means that, as often as not, some entirely futile appointments are made, for it by no means follows that because a boy is really intellectual he is morally or physically able to control a horde of boys younger than himself.

The pity of it is that mere Intellect does not command respect among boys—rather is the reverse the case. The brilliantly intellectual boy is more often than not original (an unforgivable offence in boys' eyes); he does not take the trouble to conform to what strike him as petty, irksome rules of routine; he is undisciplined and prone to kick over the traces of good taste or traditional form; he forms a small and select coterie of followers which will in all probability be very unpopular. They will discuss the poetry and prose of Decadence, the Pre-Raphaelites, Shelley, Keats, and De Quincey in their dormitories, not with understanding, much less with appreciation, but just in order to keep themselves aloof from the common herd who read, if they read at all, the *Red Magazine*, *The Premier*, or, at the highest, *Nash's*.

There is, on the other hand, the Intellectual who is acutely conscious of his shortcomings, but wishes to stand on a dignity that he does not possess, or is really anxious to inspire respect, but is possessed of none of the faculties requisite to command that most intangible and unanalysable quality.

The Intellectual has the most unenviable job of all, for it is more than likely that he will be acutely nervous of the results of his endeavours; he will be self-conscious, owing to the development of his æsthetic side, and imagine slights and failures which are in reality non-existent, whereas the merely Athletic will never be troubled by doubts, owing to his obtuseness. I must confess at once that I envy the lot of the athlete who is an athlete before all else, more than any one in the world.

He is obsessed by no troublous thoughts, as the imaginative intellectual boy is, of whether, after all, his is the best system of control. He is accustomed to lead in the games, to cajole, to drive, to encourage, riding rough-shod over any who dispute his methods, by the simple application of physical force, of which he naturally possesses a great store.

Everything is made comfortable for him. Boys and most men, constituted as they are, admire brawn and muscle, a straight eye, and a fearless tackle more than anything else. Whatever a man possessed of these qualities bids them do they do unquestioningly, only too proud to be thought worthy of notice by the demi-god. Such unthinking loyalty, amounting almost to idolatry, fosters quite naturally a feeling in the athlete's mind that he is the man who matters. The result is not only deplorable but dangerous. It leads to that quite unmistakable reaction on the part of our foremost educationists against the evils of over-athleticism on the boy while still at school. It leads to that nauseating golf, cricket, racing, and football talk which occupies the greater part of so many men's conversation to the exclusion of all else, whether it be the old public school boy in his club, or the old elementary school boy in his "pub."

Its overweening influence may be easily seen by the prodigious amount of space given over to descriptions of athletic contests by all the newspapers which pander to the tastes of their readers, and never dream of elevating the public taste even to the level of the least intellectual member of their staff.

At such a time as the present it even leads to an extraordinary amount of rubbish being talked about the "sporting" instinct of the games-ridden men who have led (as usual) in the trenches just as they led on the playing-fields. Comparisons are invidious at the best of times, but I cannot help asserting that it is my firm belief that those men of noble imagination but poor physique, poets, painters, and actors, who have answered their country's call not less certainly than the athletes, have shown themselves just as capable in the moments of stress, or when initiative of movement is required. I grant that such men feel the horror and needlessness of war more than the others who accept it all as part of the day's work, but they are surely not the less honourable for taking their share in what they consider to be a gross travesty of all human civilisation and progress because they consider that by so doing they may perhaps help to prevent any such dastardly, wanton disturbance of nature's scheme from occurring again.

It seems to me that here lies the kernel of the whole matter.

Our leaders of the future ought to be men of highly developed æsthetic taste, possessed of that vivid imagination which prompts men first of all to think of the cause of spiritual progress rather than of material success; we have too long left the affairs of the State in the hands of material-minded, selfish men.

All this "will never do." There is but one cure. You can only influence a nation as you influence an animal, by catching it young.

The present system of "prefectorial government" is ideal in theory, but we should see to it that no boy shall be allowed to lead others unless he has proved himself to be devoted to the cause of real progress, and has ideas beyond the world of school.

At present a housemaster interviews his senior boys and talks about the many "duties and privileges of prefects"; how they must not let themselves be cheapened by preserving their present friendships; at all costs they are to remember that the first essential of government is discipline; the moral and physical well-being of the house is rubbed into them, but little is said about the training of the malleable younger members to think of the vast world-wide problems upon which they will have to make up their minds so very soon and without any warning.

The root of the trouble lies in the fact that the masters themselves "never have time" to make up *their* minds about the great problems of the outside world; they take the agelong accepted opinions of their fathers, and eye with suspicious horror any theorists who dare to suggest that innovations might occasionally be beneficial to the country.

It is this stereotyped conservatism that is so dangerous a sign of the times in our great schools. Boys and masters alike are eaten up by tradition; it has become so much a religion to them that any suggestion of novel precepts is regarded as idolatry. Any young master full of enthusiasm for his programme for the regeneration of the mind of man through the public schools finds it difficult to meet with sympathy from his colleagues. He must fall into line with the rest and accept traditional customs. His idiosyncrasies, whether mere details of clothing, speech, manners or way of walking, or the greater idiosyncrasies of the mind which have developed his imagination so that he can take an interest in books or pictures or sculpture, are all food for adverse cricitism from his form or Common Room, until he finds himself suddenly outcast, a pariah, unable to achieve any of those reforms which led him to give up all for the sake of the future of the race.

But I am talking too much in the air. Baffled

as I have been on all sides in my own attempts to make people see that there is anything wrong with public schools as they are, I am in danger of becoming embittered.

Let me give you a picture of some types with whom I have come into contact, and leave you to draw your own conclusions.

I have in my mind a few actual prefects I have known.

The first, Arbuthnot, is a not over-intelligent (so far as school-work goes) member of the Shooting VIII. and Football XV., the son of a company promoter who likes to see his money's worth and is not over-pleased at his boy's repeated requests for more books. I used to see a good deal of Arbuthnot because he came to me for English essays and was an omnivorous reader. I once allowed him to ransack my library because I found, much to my surprise, for he was a popular boy, that he was intensely unhappy at school; the only outlet he had for his emotions was writing poetry, and that of a kind modelled on "The Everlasting Mercy" and "The Widow in the Bye-Street." I did not wish to drive him away from books altogether by suddenly substituting Milton for the more lurid poets who had attracted him, but it was an extraordinarily arduous business diverting him from the moderns, the contributors to "The Yellow Book," back to the calm majesty of the classics.

He was a wild devotee of debates here; having assimilated the notions of Shaw and others, he would delight to throw bombs about in the most careless manner. This caused him to gain a certain notoriety, as a result of which he became editor of a flagrant publication entitled *The Hornet*, which nearly brought about his instant expulsion: the lampoons upon the staff were never forgiven, and he became more and more harassed by his house and other masters until he implored his father to take him away. He became a prefect for two terms before he left, but never took the trouble either to keep order or to preserve that sense of dignity in himself which it is of the first importance that prefects should cultivate. In consequence he was by a strange anomaly beloved in his "house," and when he started to "rag" the house games, the spirit of revolt against athletics spread like wildfire and he became a sort of god among the smaller fry.

It was not until he had actually left school and been at Cambridge for a year that he came to see how foolish his conduct at school had been: it was a sort of kicking against the pricks with no adequate purpose: he had been unhappy for no very cogent reason, and had wreaked his vengeance on a school which would not take the trouble to find out where one individual member was being unwittingly rubbed up the wrong way. As a prefect his influence, which might have been and should have been excellent, was malign: it took the house at least a year to recover its prestige in the eyes of the rest of the school: it had become slack, lost its sense of esprit de corps, and gone in for crankiness and the cult of foolishness.

Another prefect I have in mind is Howard. He also is the head of a house, devoutly religious, a Philistine in thought and intellect, an indomitable worker at school subjects, because he knows that he must get a scholarship if he wishes ever to get to Cambridge, a strong athlete by reason of continued plodding rather than by any natural genius, and a rigid disciplinarian. He has no difficulty with his house, no doubt about his success; he is the "model boy," held up to admiration on Speech Days, the recipient of many prizes, an inexhaustible source of joy (and incidentally a wonderful saver of trouble) to his housemaster.

Years hence we shall talk of him with bated breath as "that wonderful boy Howard" who rescued a house which was going to rack and ruin, established it on sound lines, and kept it going entirely "off his own bat"—and quite rightly. He is a valuable product.

Then there is Watson, the great spectacled classical scholar—nervous, futile, hideous. You see him in every school. From his earliest days at his first private school he has been trained in the classics very much as a prize Pomeranian is trained for the shows. He goes through his public school exactly as a prize dog would. Nothing matters except the assimilation of the classics—eternal Latin and Greek. He never derives any ghost of an idea as to what it all means. The æsthetic joys only to be gained from the Greeks are hidden from him; he is mentally blind; he no more enjoys his food than the dog does—he takes it because it is good for him. In the end, he goes to Balliol, after years of incompetence at school, where he has been the "butt" of the Lower School; he takes (perhaps) a First in "Greats," and returns to vomit the undigested masses of the classics which he has stored up to other boys of a later generation, and continues to be the "butt" of his form for the rest of his life, until he dies "unwept, unhonoured, and unsung"—a pitiable tragedy. Is such a man likely to influence a malleable generation for good? I think not.

I have taken up too much space already with these types. Let me conclude with one more friend of mine—Herbertson.

He is fairly athletic, tremendously keen on all the problems of the day, possessed of a liberal intelligence, anxious only to develop his intellect, so that he may be the better able to take an unbiased view of life, and so help to the best of his ability suffering humanity. Consequently he reads omnivorously all the poetry, history, novels, and sociological works that he can lay his hands on.

This does not endear him to the rest of the house, who talk of games to the exclusion of all else. In a house match he will play a brilliant game; but the night after, if any one starts to comment on it, his usual remark is, "Oh, for God's sake, shut up!"

His path is made as difficult for him as possible,

both by his housemaster and juniors, who, like all unimaginative people, hate what they do not understand.

It is useless to elaborate further. I have given you fair specimens in existing circumstances, and leave it to your judgment. The question is · "Is all well as we stand?" I am far too much of an optimist to think so. Hence my cry from the housetops until I make the people hear. It is the only means left, so puny seem my own personal efforts as an assistant master in a big school.

At times I get so dispirited at the attacks that are made upon my "loyalty," my "upsetting, irrational, nonsensical notions," that I feel inclined to let things slide, to acquiesce, and be comfortable; on such occasions the only weapon left me is my pen—so, with my lance in rest, I go on tilting at windmills.

CHAPTER XII

SCHOOL MAGAZINES

A SCHOOL magazine to be successful must be of illegitimate birth.

The school "mag," as the official organ is usually called, is too heavily censored, as becomes "official organs," to reflect the real opinion of the school on any point of local importance; the writer has to take into account what the headmaster, housemasters, and all the staff think before he dare put forward a new theory. There is always lurking at the back of his mind the fearful thought that he may be committing a grave breach of etiquette in propounding a fresh theory about compulsory games, attendance in chapel, the validity of certain old-established traditions and unwritten laws: he may be accused of treachery, disloyalty, lack of esprit de corps, and suffer accordingly both from those in power and his friends.

Consequently, to be on the safe side, an editor of a school magazine permits of nothing but accounts of games, concerts, field days, dramatic performances, debates, letters from the Front, and a harmless verse or so, translated from the

Greek, with the result that the finished number is so tedious as to bore every one to tears except the smaller fry and the ambitious, who rush to see their names in print as having distinguished themselves on the field of play or on the platform.

Were it not part of the school's laws that every boy perforce has to subscribe sixpence per number towards the production of these periodicals, most of them would have ceased to exist through lack of funds shortly after their inception. Old Boys, masters, and present Winchburians alike always complain as each number appears that it is only duller than the last.

Once having satisfied themselves that their names do or do not appear, their interest vanishes at once.

And it should in fairness be understood at once that it is not for lack of talent that these journals fail; in every school there are many really brilliant writers who never even approach the editor with their MSS., knowing full well that unless they say what is trite and commonplace their "stuff" stands no chance of acceptance.

It is in consequence of this that enthusiastic waves of literary endeavour from time to time take place, and for a short space of time really brilliant ephemeral periodicals flit into our ken, only to disappear all too soon.

These secret, short-lived bursts are sometimes astonishingly full of genius, and after all who can wonder? These are those illegitimate expressions of a boy's soul—

> " Which in the lusty stealth of Nature, take
> More composition and fierce quality
> Than doth . . . go to the creating of a whole tribe of
> 'mags'
> Got 'tween asleep and wake!"

I remember in my own schooldays that as a counter-attraction to the official *Crantonian* we ran a rival called *The Critic*. This magazine, which was illustrated and uncensored, was read aloud fortnightly on alternate Sunday evenings to the delighted members of a club called the Junior Debating Society. There was but one copy, and the editor was a boy of fine literary taste. We criticised everything—masters, prefects, customs, games, abuses—with a freedom that has been denied us ever since in a world where the law of libel holds us up at every turn; never again have any of us been allowed to say exactly what we mean or to indulge in such sharp, biting, vituperative language. We boldly copied Swift and Pope, Byron and Dryden; our couplets and epigrams were bandied about from month to month for terms; we felt ourselves among the immortals; we were coiners of phrases which outlasted our time; we invented nicknames that still stick, twenty years after. What greater fame could man desire?

And still can we con with delight our own unformed writing if we choose to go back to Cranton and poke about in the archives of the

Junior Debating Society Library, for every copy of *The Critic* was kept and bound.

The secret of our success? No censor, no dread of public opinion. All contributions were anonymous; also, most important of all, we were paid according to merit. The pride that thrills a boy on first receiving a piece of silver, ay, even sometimes of gold, for his own writing is finer than any other sensation in life.

Since those days I have had to act as contributor, reader, censor, and editor to many magazines, but I have never met with truer self-expression, better satire, or such good-humoured chaff as in those old days of *The Critic*.

I remember once in later years that a certain house noted for its tendency towards literary expression at Harchester started a rival to the *Harcastrian* called *The Wasp*. Its first and last editor was a boy-poet who is now among the more famous of the younger school of Georgian poets. It was an amazing *tour de force*. The editor wrote practically the whole magazine from cover to cover. It was typed and cost sixpence a copy. There were plays in blank verse modelled on Stephen Phillips, passionate love-poems obviously based on Ernest Dowson and Swinburne, attacks on stereotyped religions, forms, and ceremonies, gems of fairy poetry distinctly reminiscent of Walter de la Mare, fantastic stories of mystery and imagination founded on Richard Middleton and Edgar Allan Poe, long narrative poems full of obscenities showing the influence of " The Everlasting Mercy " and " The Widow in the Bye-Street"—all the great writers of yesterday and to-day were exploited ruthlessly to provide copy for their disciples at Harchester. The strange part of the whole magazine was that there was never a word about the school; no attempt at abuse, no scurrilous condemnation of the *Harcastrian*, no flighty satire about masters' ways, masters' dress, masters' incompetence.

I think it was this very aloofness that so irritated the headmaster when once, by chance, he happened to see a copy.

Full of rage, he sent for the editor; he demanded that all copies should be burnt, and was only prevented from instantly expelling the unfortunate editor after a stand-up fight with the boy's housemaster. He could not see that this self-expression was not "immoral," as he stigmatised it, at all, but rather was a very powerful safety-valve for the outpouring of the emotions of a few highly-strung boys who craved for something more than they found in the hide-bound routine and monotony of school life.

I have kept all copies of *The Wasp*. Some day the world will probably thank me for having done so, to judge from the way in which young J—— A——'s later work is now selling.

I have before me now two new productions of two separate cliques at Winchborough.

The one, *The Castigator*, costs threepence, is advertised to appear monthly, and is badly printed off from the Army Side master's "jellygraph" at infinite cost of trouble and time.

It is a strange periodical.

It opens with a sonnet which I cannot forbear from quoting; it shows the new spirit, brought about by the war, at work, and is most distinctly poetry.

"THE CALL

'Lusimus satis: tempus est abire'

As the spring morn casts off its winter raiment
So put we by the garb that we have worn
Draggled through many wanderings, and torn
By passions that demand their bitter payment
Of the Gods' golden gift of Youth and Love.
Now stand we strong of heart and clear of eye
And they remain only in memory,—
Those fevered days that now seem so far off.

For the word England like a flame was breathed,
And we forgot the old desires and joys,
The barren ecstasies and clamouring noise
Of pleasure. Then with penitential awe
Mingled with proud thanksgiving, our eyes saw
The sword of Honour and The Faith unsheathed."

So fine a start is, naturally enough, not sustained; that were too much to expect.

The editorial, like nearly all editorials, is poor; its only merit is its brevity. It is stilted and self-conscious; altogether too boyish.

Then follows "News of the House," which is, of course, of local interest, and panders to that taste which likes to see its name in print, even in "jellygraph" print, and this is succeeded by an extraordinary story about China which would not disgrace the pen of such an authority as Mr. J. O. P. Bland.

After this we are prepared for anything. We are not surprised to find a serial not unlike those of Miss Ruby M. Ayres, which *The Times* chooses to boom so freely for its sister, the *Daily Mirror*; there is the inevitable ghost story, some bad verses on a school abuse, a vast quantity of quite amusing correspondence, a series of "howlers" committed by members of the house in form (a gorgeous page of self-revelations), and the fourteenth page sees the last of "No. 1, Vol. I."

All success to it, say I; this is what we want.

I have before me the first copy of a new Winchburian production, printed by the local photographer, called *The Clarion*, price 2d. Let me say at once that it is by far the best school magazine I have ever seen. It is conducted in absolute secrecy, even to the point of being delivered in a sealed envelope. It contains nothing which could possibly betray the authorship of any one contribution.

On the first page we read that:

"*The Clarion* is the first innovation here for years, and perhaps the only thing at Winchborough which is not compulsory."

Later:

"One of the many merits of *The Clarion* is that it contains no articles on public schools in war-time."

Later again:

"Do not imagine that *The Clarion* is produced by masters—it is far too clever.

"It has no tales of classic fights
By military nuts;
No deft debaters wronging rights,
No rising to poetic heights,
No lays of literary lights,
Or chronicles of 'guts.'"

There follows an extremely able "hit" at the "Bloods," called "Etiquette in the Upper Circle." One of the most bitter rules for candidates is No. 3:

"Candidates must be careful to avoid all important questions when conversing. Conversation should be confined to games, the weather, and the work you haven't done, and should always be of a light and humorous character when not abusive."

A real sense of poetry is reached in "The Wood," which begins:

"At the shadowed hour of midnight, in the dark-leaved forest reaches,
When the lonely little moonbeams flicker struggling through the beeches,
When the tiny, mournful breezes with a moaning and a sighing
Through the swaying, whispering branches come a-creaking and a-crying . . .
Then the wicked little people of the forest are a-gadding,
With their little eyes a-twinkle and their little feet a-padding."

This is followed up by some remarkably apposite correspondence in which a plea for less extravagant energy in games is put forward "now that the school is in a better condition, morally and socially, than it has ever been before."

An unmerciful parody of the first four pages of the current number of *The Winchburian* paves the way for the bon-mot of the number.

This is a jest almost too good to be true. The editor of *The Winchburian* one day received a letter purporting to emanate from an old boy, R. E. Mydleton, who desired to print two sonnets in the forthcoming issue. The editor replied that he was unable to accede to this request unless Mr. Mydleton would specify exactly when he was at Winchborough This the author, in his reply, stated that he was unable to do as he had changed his name, and dare not disclose a secret which would cause pain to one who was dear to him. The editor, in remorse, agreed to print the sonnets, and wrote a most touching letter of apology for his first harsh note. Judge of his horror when he discovered that on the very day that he received the second letter from Mr. Mydleton, that unfortunate poet had died. In the *Daily Mail* of 13th November 1915 appeared this obituary notice

"MYDLETON.—Very suddenly, on Wednesday evening, at Cambridge Square, Hyde Park, RALPH E. MYDLETON, the poet, aged fifty-one."

Of course the whole thing was a hoax. The sonnets, which incidentally had appeared already in *The Winchburian* a short time before, were ridiculously bad; there never had been a Mr. Mydleton—and the editor of *The Winchburian* is now like the immortal Partridge of almanack fame in Swift's day, the butt of inextinguishable laughter.

The Clarion publishes the whole correspondence and somewhat naturally gloats over its unfortunate contemporary.

"And so," runs the indictment, "the editor of *The Winchburian* believes that by refusing to accept Mr. Mydleton's sonnets he has made himself the virtual murderer of this unfortunate and mysterious contributor."

Such a "scoop" for the opening number of a school magazine it would be hard to rival. It stands alone among the schoolboy jests of our time.

Long may *The Clarion* and its kind flourish. Led by such a spirit of literary adventure its contributors are well on the way to train themselves to become writers who will really matter in the next generation, and we sadly need a training-school for the young journalist before he casts off the fetters of discipline which Winchborough and other such places so beneficially provide for the genius of to-morrow.

CHAPTER XIII

GAMES

ONE of the greatest benefits which the war has conferred upon us is the depreciation of the value of athletics consequent upon the rise of the corps.

We were in grave danger of falling into the snare of making success in the games one of the first standards by which we judged our fellow-men. A " Blue " was always safe to be offered a post at most public schools, regardless of his qualities as a master. The theory was that boys would naturally reverence a man who had the magic gift of a straight eye or an abnormal wind.

As a matter of fact, boys were not so easily hoodwinked. Some of the worst masters we have ever known have been " Blues "—men without brains, without a sense of humour or proportion, with no sense of dignity or discipline, useless in every walk of life except on the running track or on the river.

Our daily papers did their best to lend colour to the fact that England's gods were her professional cricket and football players by giving up whole pages to accounts of games all over the country.

War has changed all that. We still play games, but we play them, not work at them now. But two years ago and every game seemed to be degenerating into a science which required years of incessant and arduous practice. The whole point of a game is that it should be relaxation. To play hard is one thing, to play in such a state of nervous tension that you go "stale" in half a term is another—and tends to ruin all the good that undoubtedly accrues from healthy exercise.

There was a time, not long ago, when boys could be got to talk of nothing else but their chances of getting caps, the chances of their houses in the cup-ties, the probable choices for the first and second Fifteens and Elevens. That talk has now luckily been diverted into a healthier channel; the O.T.C. takes up much more of their time and occupies their thoughts, to the partial exclusion of games. But still games are played, and there is a tendency as the war goes on to revert to the old false values.

Boys come tired out and listless into afternoon school after a strenuous practice, and for all the good they derive from the lesson might as well be asleep in their studies.

The truth is, that even now the average boy is driven too much; every one knows that it is bad for the young to have too much time to himself, but I am not sure that it is not an equally bad thing for him to have no time to himself. From bed he is hurried to physical training, from physical training to breakfast, from breakfast to chapel, and then to work for four hours on end, which may be, in a slack form, his only rest for the day. As soon as he comes out of school he is drilled in the O.T.C., a hurried lunch is followed by a scramble into football clothes, and he is hounded up and down the fields for an hour by his house captain under pretence of being kept fit. Back he goes to his house with just time to change before afternoon school; by the time that 6.15 comes he is ready to drop through sheer fatigue. Tea is followed at once by preparation, supper and more preparation, and at ten o'clock he is rushed to bed, having had no instant to himself since he got up in the early morning.

Now a "slack" afternoon every now and again would just be the saving of him. Every boy ought to be allowed two afternoons in the week "off" games, when he should be permitted to go off on his bicycle, walk, play golf, slack in his study, or do whatever he pleased to counteract the effect of the other days. Only so can games be made the pleasurable relaxation which they were meant to be. There is too much giving of colours and choosing of sides, too much excitement to go "all out" all the time, day in, day out, throughout the term. A day with beagles, a run to hounds once every fortnight would do everybody a world of good. It would take them out of the narrow routine, they would meet fresh people, see fresh scenes, become, as all lovers of the hunt become, lovers of nature.

There is a section of society which looks askance at boys daring to go down to the playing-fields in football garb at all; they say that it shows a levity sadly out of place at a time when all the nation's energies should be expended on one object alone—the conquest of the enemy by whatever means.

Such people forget, what all unthinking opponents of games forget, that if you are to train a man for any post of intellectual or moral responsibility you must keep him physically fit, and that you can do this in no better way than by encouraging him to play in games that encourage the team spirit.

Most of the qualities that make for the good soldier are learnt in the games; courage, self-reliance, quickness to seize the initiative, calm determination to do one's best whatever the issue: all these are taught quicker and more effectively on the cricket and football field than anywhere else.

It is only when these things are treated as a fetish that games fail. It is all a question of μηδὲν ἄγαν. Scarcely any boy ever overworks,—no boy knows how to,—whereas nearly every boy overplays, and in addition to the resulting loss of balance in his mind he usually overstrains some organ of his body which may render him physically useless at twenty-five. What else can you expect after witnessing even a Junior House match? You have never seen one? Let me try and depict one for you.

Imagine a filthy afternoon in mid-February,

a wild waste of mud-flats, four hundred boys in corps boots, heavy overcoats, mufflers, and (strange incongruity) straw hats, slowly filtering past a gaunt, elderly pedagogue who snappishly calls over the roll from a little blue book which, by the time he reaches the Lower School, is saturated with rain and mud.

A mad scamper follows to the lower grounds where the first round of the Juniors is to be played to-day. For weeks each side has been training down to the last hair—getting up at unholy hours in the early morning, refusing all invitations to tea from kindly masters' wives (who are all unwitting of the temptation they offer by their untimely advances), meticulously careful about their diet in Hall, eschewing all sweet-stuffs and potatoes, all fat-forming material that comes their way. Here they are at last brought to the test, all nervous, uttering the most inane remarks to any one who will listen, in a manner quite foreign to them.

The referee whistles: blazers, sweaters, and caps of honour are discarded, and the teams take the field, each individual unconsciously deploring his lack of muscle and inches when compared with any of the opposing side, who seem to have grown immense in the night. They line up; a hand is held up aloft, the ball is kicked away down the ground, a frenzied mêlée ensues—the match has begun. Wild cheers from the spectators for "Raleigh's" or "Bradley's" cease not now for eighty minutes, except for breathing-space at half-time. Here are collected Yeomanry officers, masters and their wives, local tradespeople and day boys' parents, and some few strangers interspersed among the wild horde of boys who race violently up and down the touch-line imploring their House to " use your *feet*, fee-eet—fee-eet—man, fee-eet——" " Pass threes, pass, can't you ? " " Well played, laddies! Well played, boys!"—this in a frenzied tone from one of the house-masters who, clad in white shorts and stockings and an old Cambridge blazer, is tearing up and down the field, megaphone to his mouth, for all the world like a river " coach " on the banks by Long Bridges. The other housemaster interested is lean, taciturn, and aged; neatly dressed in bowler hat and a brown suit, he stands cynically surveying the scene from behind the goal-post, saying to himself in a continued undertone, "Good old House! Well played, House!" But aloud, when any one ventures to approach him, will veer away from the match altogether and discuss the lights on the trees over Honey-mead or Crowcombe Hill.

This particular match to-day seems to be of an extraordinary character, for Raleigh's, with only thirteen men, lead at half-time (mainly owing to the exertions of their gesticulating housemaster, it is true) by 14 points to nil; in the second " half," however, their weakness in numbers tells—gradually the points are piled up until the score rises, amidst maddening excitement, to 14 points all. Immediately after, the whistle blows "No side." "Will they play on?"

The captains of the respective houses confer—Raleigh's chieftain most emphatically declining to hear of any more to-day. With his thirteen men he is only too glad to have made a tie of it. "We'll replay next week."

The manager of school games wanders up to the circle where the argument waxes hot and furious, and informs them that they must play on, five minutes each way. The teams look at each other, every man piteously wondering how soon it will be before he faints; the strain has already bereft him of all strength or thoughts. Somehow they hang on, scarcely moving in the mud and slime: half-time, no score; another age-long five minutes, and still no score—Over, thank God! for the day. And so the concourse breaks up, only to fight the entire match over again in Common Room, in the tuck shop, in the studies, to dissent from the games manager's decision, to rebel against that last try which the referee allowed, to describe momentary gleams of greatness, to dilate on the rottenness of Bradley's "halves," and so on; while the poor, unfortunate players simply go on training, waiting more nervous than ever for the replay of this titanic struggle.

This is not how we would have our games travestied: I have said enough. Now is the time, before professionalism becomes paramount, to eradicate for ever any taint of professionalism in our schools.

CHAPTER XIV

THE TEMPORARY MASTER

THIS is an age in which all education stands a good chance of being neglected altogether; on the one hand, we hear of salaries being docked in the elementary schools just at a time when it is becoming increasingly hard for a teacher to afford even the bare necessaries of life, and impossible for him to meet the new taxation; on the other hand, screamers in every paper, who are busying themselves trying to stop every industry and profession in order that men may be found fit to fight, have been querulously asking why education is permitted to go on: What good does it do? What return do we see for our money?

The public schools have wonderfully settled down to work under war conditions; deprived of all their more responsible elder boys the younger ones have stepped into the breach, and are acquitting themselves splendidly as heads of houses, captains of games, presidents of societies, and prefects of school; work, games, the O.T.C., every department of school life is not only keeping up its old tradition of efficiency, but steadily improving on the old standards.

Perhaps the place where we have suffered most since the Christmas term of 1914 has been in the ranks of the Common Room.

The older housemasters, of course, mountain-like, remain steadfast; but there has been sad havoc wrought in the type of younger assistant master.

We have lost all who were eligible for war, and have had to reconstitute the staff as best we could out of the stuff left on the agents' books.

First of all, we roped in all the very old men who had given up work years ago, masters of an age-long past, stern taskmasters, who asked and gave no quarter, who knew, like Dr. Johnson, that all they had learnt had been beaten into them with the cane.

Valiantly they responded to the call to come and help; they are still with us, men of decided opinions, not only about "all this hotch-potch of modern education which fits a boy to become nothing better than a crossing-sweeper," but who openly deride their younger (and, incidentally, senior) colleagues on their attitude towards, and relationships with, the boys under their charge: "All this bridging of the chasm, you know, it won't do—so much soft soap . molly-coddling, favouritism, tut-tut . . . fallacy of the elder brother . . . disgusting, effeminate . . .," and so on.

Tolerantly we smile; in secret we laugh at these adherents of "the good old days"; but no one can say that we do not envy these men their glorious self-possession, their amazing assurance that they are indubitably right, while we scatter like a bad pack of hounds after every sort of scent in our frenzy to pick up the right trail of that elusive fox, liberal education; each of us pioneer-like baying to high heaven that we and we alone have found out the right path, inciting all the other hounds to follow us in the pursuit, only to lose all traces of our quarry at the first obstacle.

And yet in our heart of hearts we know that we are right, that in spite of our dismal and all too frequent failures we are more likely to evolve a scheme of true education than these stereotyped town-criers with their "Aut classics (*sic!*) aut nihil" ever dreamed of. The days of rigid movements in a fixed line are over; we of the twentieth century are as averse from the very sound of the word "groove" as our forefathers of the eighteenth were from "enthusiasm"; if we cannot indulge in hyperbolic flights we prefer not to move at all; we become barristers, not schoolmasters.

A second type of temporary master that the war has called into being is the very young, much-bespectacled, physically unfit, but intellectually brilliant scholar. In normal times this type would become a don immediately after taking a degree; but as "Othello's occupation's gone," with regard to the nourishing of the mind of the searcher after a "First in Greats," he has to descend to the level of the black abysmal ignorance of the Middle School. As a result he is at first hopelessly lost; his lessons are so much above the heads of his hearers as to be dubbed by them " bally hot-air," " the meanderings of a freak." . . . This type has to learn that the public school boy does not wish to improve ; his first object is to make out of what stuff his " beaks " are made. If, in his anxiety to impress on the soul of youth the importance of and lasting benefits that accrue from hard work, he forgets that he has first to insist on the strictest discipline, he is lost, irrecoverably lost.

There are many good honest souls who would have us believe that, because there is a war on, boys are no longer boys ; that they have suddenly become quietened, chastened, angelic. No bigger mistake could possibly be made. The youth of to-day is just as willing to take advantage of weakness, either in the new, nervous weakling in his house, whom he bullies with as much gusto as ever, or in the type of master which I have just depicted. Ink is still upset down the backs of unfortunate new boys in the classrooms of such men ; paper is still thrown gloriously about the form in sheer abandonment of spirits, while careful geometrical figures are being drawn on the board by " the char " (I should explain that all temporary " ushers " are politely included in one comprehensive, expressive phrase : " The Chars ") ; hideous noises of groaning, cheers, hisses, stampings of feet, explosions, ghastly smells, live animals, and so on, still emanate from the classrooms where these men are supposed to be teaching. It is all very tragic, albeit very natural.

Here are men only too willing to give of their best to do their country service, refused the privilege of taking up arms for the cause, who turn to education, knowing full well how important it is that the youth of to-day should be well served in the present crisis ; men, full of culture and ideas, only too anxious to propagate their learning and perpetuate their theories of an ideal state, who find themselves, instead of seeing their castles in the air materialise before their eyes, confronted by brute beasts in the mass, hungry for their blood, caring nothing whatever for ideals and sound learning, on the look out only for a slip on the part of the master that they may roar, get out of hand, and convert themselves into a set of unmanageable pigs, lowest of breathing animals. How I should like to bring down some of those men who think that the public schools can be run by any type of man while its finest and best spirits are liberated to fight in Flanders or the Dardanelles, to see a school in the working under its present grievous handicap !

They would talk no more of that sort of cant which we too frequently hear, that "any sort of ass can be a successful schoolmaster."

We, as a race, have been maligned too long ; we have borne only too patiently the affronts of men of letters who ought to have known the truth. Kipling and his betters have all kicked us to gain popularity : we want no man's praises, but we sometimes sigh for justice.

The art of teaching is not one that can be

learnt in a day: æstheticism, brain-power, idealism, passionate fervour alone count for nothing; a man must be able to handle boys before he can teach them anything.

A third class of master, a direct product of the war, now swims into our ken—the wounded hero. Armless, legless, disabled permanently as a soldier, such a man may yet make a magnificent schoolmaster.

To begin with, he has an overwhelming advantage over all other men from the very start. Boys quite naturally reverence a man who has actually been face to face with death and narrowly missed it. Such a man will have already been practised in the art of discipline; having handled men, he ought to be able, unless he is a prodigious fool, to handle boys without difficulty. Having endured the horrors of war, he will, to use a phrase of Carlyle's, have cleared his mind of cant, and as a consequence have much to say on the conduct of life which boys will believe all the more readily when they see from his face that his statements are no mere commonplaces of doctrine, but fundamental facts learnt only by dreadful experience; his theories, having been purified seven times in the fire, will carry an air of verisimilitude which is only too often lacking in the theories which we attempt to impose on the youthful mind.

Particularly in the teaching of history, English literature, and the classics, will such men be found of great use; for no one is quicker to detect insincerity in writing or quicker to gain inspiration from real genius than the schoolboy when properly trained, and the soldier who has undergone the baptism of fire. The one will react upon the other; the soldier will fix upon those passages in the works of the great masters which most helped him in the hour of need, and will impress upon his form the lifelong satisfaction and solace that are to be derived from such sources, if only they are read with the imaginative faculties sharpened, and ready to absorb their benign influences.

The help that such men can render in the training of the Officers' Training Corps is so obvious as to need no comment.

There seems to be much talk about the future of many of our wounded officers who will, owing to the severity of their wounds, be unable to pursue the vocations which knew them before the war.

Surely here is a solution. Even now every school in the land is crying out for masters, temporary in many cases; but that word "temporary" now will mean in only too many schools "permanent," for how few of our soldier-schoolmasters will ever come back alive gives us furiously to think. The usual supply annually taken from the universities has now absolutely dried up. As a consequence, men are now taking two, three, four times the number of boys, and doing two, three, four times as much work as they did before the war. They must have relief if education matters at all.

Here is the chance of the permanently disabled

officer: he need not think that his life is at an end because he has lost an arm or a leg. Let him come to us and take his share in forming the opinions and shaping the character of the England of to-morrow; it is no light job; it is an intensely patriotic and important one.

Life is going to be none too easy for the youth of to-day when it grows up to be the man of to-morrow. There are going to be problems to be solved which will call for the best-developed brains, the highest moral qualities, a steadfastness of aim and immobility of purpose that need cultivating at once if they are to be achieved.

Your fight is not yet over, O soldier-hero! Come once more into the lists; your physical battles have made you finer men than we are; come among us and share the spiritual conflict, so that when old age comes upon us, and we are about to die, both of us may look back on the past years and say: "According to our lights we did our best: the England of to-day is better than the England of yesterday; this we helped to bring about; our lives have not been entirelv purposeless."

CHAPTER XV

THE HOLIDAY TASK

I SUPPOSE that the words "Holiday Tasks" never connoted any such real, living, serious *work* as they do now. In the past we inevitably conjured up visions of books to be read, notes to be taken, exercises to be worked out, and so on.

Now we are one and all intent upon spending ourselves to the full, not in revising Æschylus and Sophocles, Taylor's theorem or mediæval European history, but in manual labour, in military work, in helping, so far as in us lies, to carry on the work of the country wherever we may be found useful.

Nor is it the schoolboy alone who is devoting himself voluntarily to the new kind of holiday task; the masters, too, in their own particular ways, are giving up their much-longed-for weeks of rest in order to be of some service to the nation.

Elderly priests are taking parish work in Scotland or the Lakes in order to set free younger clergymen who wish to make munitions or indulge in other forms of active service.

The music masters are bound for Y.M.C.A. tents in military centres where their vocal and musical faculties generally are only too sorely needed; housemasters with big families are going *en masse* to take over farms in Suffolk, Kent, Devon, and Cornwall, so that they may assist in the harvest and general farm work for seven weeks; senior officers in the O.T.C., captains and majors, are drafted into regiments where they can train the newer subalterns; the junior officers are willing to undertake the instruction of Kitchener's Third Line of Home Defence, for two months to go through all the drudgery of squad and platoon drill in which they are so adequately versed here at school. Less agile and less physically fit members of the staff have signed on as army workers in London, Southampton, Edinburgh, Inverness, outlying villages in Wales, and thickly congested districts of Lancashire.

Others, again, who wish to prove how muscular their bodies are, and to what extent their powers of endurance can last, have applied successfully for jobs in mines, or as goods porters on all the principal railways; scientists have been permitted to tackle intricate pieces of engineering, while the more sedentary have been selected for clerical work connected with the Red Cross Inquiry as to the whereabouts of missing soldiers, expressing their willingness to be sent from hospital to hospital all over the kingdom in their search, or to sit in an office day after day and write letters to anxious relatives with regard to whatever information they have gleaned from wounded friends about their missing loved ones.

The elder boys, of course, are only too delighted now that the fetters of school are loosened and their age has advanced to the limit required for commissions in the Army. After a year of chafing, their delight at being at last allowed to do something is unbounded. Their quite natural and usually overpowering sorrow at leaving school and the friends of years is now more than counterbalanced by the splendid anticipation of immediate military activity.

Looking through the school list, it would appear at first sight that no boy worth counting was coming back next term; but that thought oppresses us regularly every year at this time, war or no war, so that goes for nothing. Those returning, as a matter of fact, include many quite elderly boys who are unable, through physical defects, to enter the Army.

Of these many are now employed as sergeants or corporals on the East Coast; they are living in tents on the same fare as the ordinary soldier, and are acting as sergeant-instructors, and marvellously well are they acquitting themselves in these posts, though they are of no light responsibility

I even know of some sixteen-year-olds who have prevailed upon their patriotic parents to permit them to spend the summer at Hendon, where they may learn the rudiments of flying, so that next year they may enter the Royal Flying Corps, the *Ultima Thule* of every young boy's ambitions.

What a difference war has made in these, our

self-imposed holiday tasks! Somehow we no longer talk of books, and yet just as many are packed, just as many are taken away, just as many are read—yes, read, but in how different a spirit from formerly! Both boys and masters will be reading these holidays—just as deep and abstruse literature as ever, but how much more carefully, with how much more zest and interest.

After a hard day's route march, or gathering in of corn, or of coal-heaving, or of tackling any job of national importance, how infinitely greater and more instant will be the appeal of the majestic Greek poet, of the English playwright, or of the philosopher! What a welcome change will be the delicate mathematical problem, the analysing of that chemical compound!

The admixture of bodily energy with intellectual effort will make these holidays for ever after a precious memory, physique and brain will each receive an added stimulus, and, more important than all, think how the moral side of each of us is likely to be affected.

Think of the example we are setting to those with whom we are now brought into contact—the professional coal-heavers, the regular goods porter, the farm-hand, the city clerk, the soldiers, whether in tent or canteen. We of the public schools have held only too long aloof from the life of the country. Now, through the agency of war, will the Cavendish Association be able to point to us and say, "Did I not always tell you so? Does not salvation come through Personal, Social, Christian Service?" The mingling of all classes in this common endeavour will make for a better understanding between classes, will go a long way to remove all that bitterness of feeling which arises from suspicion and lack of knowledge of the aims of other strata of society than our own.

The public school boy will no longer sneer at his less fortunate companion of the streets; the illiberally educated will no longer hate the supercilious superiority, no longer shrink under the contempt of the richer, the more intellectual, the nobler born among his countrymen.

England is on the right path; we need not fear for her future. Still shall we be able to boast with Wordsworth, "In everything we are sprung Of Earth's first blood, have titles manifold"; ay, and bear it in mind as a motto to live up to, so that in the years to come we may look back on this difficult era as a time when we first recognised this truth and, owing to God's grace, did nothing to tarnish England's good name, but rather, in so far as we were able, consummated our ambition of bringing men nearer to each other and nearer to God.

The above chapter was written immediately before one such "war holiday," hence the use of the present and future tenses.

CHAPTER XVI

GALLERY OF SCHOOLMASTERS

"   a time, sixty summers ago,
When, a young, chubby chap, I sat just so
With others on a school-form rank'd in a row,
With intelligences agape and eyes aglow,
While an authoritative old wiseacre
Stood over us, and from a desk fed us with flies.

.   .   .

A dry biped he was, nurtured likewise
On skins and skeletons, stale from top to toe
With all manner of rubbish and all manner of lies."

ROBERT BRIDGES.

NOT long ago I received an invitation to attend a meeting of a celebrated Literary Society at one of our great public schools where a paper was read on "The Schoolmaster in Literature," during the course of which the reader remarked that it was a curious and very unpleasant coincidence that all authors had, through all the ages, combined in a sort of conspiracy to malign and caricature a noble profession. This set me thinking, and first I must say bluntly that I am in this instance at any rate a believer in the well-worn adage, that "Where there is smoke fire cannot be far distant." A certain substratum of truth underlies all that the literary lights of our land have to say concerning the pedagogue, and it is undeniable that not only in fiction but in real life people instinctively avoid the society of schoolmasters, however charming they may be, at least for a little. There is a distinct aversion to be conquered in the minds of most men before they will take the members of this profession to their bosoms.

There is, however, a theory that I wish to promulgate: it is that the geniuses of letters have not in the past been so wrong as the present-day schoolmaster would like to think. Thomas Fuller, in *The Holy State and the Profane State*, has some illuminating comments on the schoolmaster of his time:

"There is scarce any profession in the Commonwealth more necessary which is so slightly performed The reasons whereof I conceive to be these: First, Young scholars make this calling their refuge; yea, perchance, before they have taken any degree in the University, commence schoolmasters in the country, as if nothing else were required to set up this profession but only a rod and a ferula. Secondly, Others who are able, use it only as a passage to better preferment, to patch the rents in their present fortune, till they can provide a new one, and betake themselves to some more gainful calling. Thirdly, They are disheartened from doing their best with the miserable reward which in some places they receive, being masters to the children, and slaves to the parents.

Fourthly, Being grown rich, they grow negligent, and scorn to touch the school but by the proxy of the usher. But see how well our (fictitious) schoolmaster behaves himself.

"1. His genius inclines him with delight to his profession.

"2. He studieth his scholars' natures as carefully as they their books, and separateth them into these divisions:

"(*a*) Those that are ingenious and industrious. Such natures he useth with all gentleness.

"(*b*) Those that are ingenious and idle. Oh! a good rod will finely take them napping.

"(*c*) Those that are dull and diligent. That schoolmaster deserves to be beaten himself who beats nature in a boy for a fault.

"(*d*) Those that are invincibly dull and negligent also. Such boys he consigneth over to other professions. Those may make excellent merchants and mechanics which will not serve for scholars."

The man who calls negroes "images of God cut in ebony," will not make a mistake through lack of sympathy when he describes the schoolmasters of his age; so we may be sure that much of the above, which reads as if it were written this year, will be found to be a correct estimate of the mid-seventeenth-century pedagogue.

Next to Fuller I would take Dr. Johnson, a peculiarly valuable witness, for he suffered both as a boy from other masters, and as a man from inside experience. For a time he was one of us. Of one of his masters (Mr. Hunter of Lichfield) he says : " He was very severe, and wrong-headedly severe. He used to beat us unmercifully ; and he did not distinguish between ignorance and negligence, for he would beat a boy equally for not knowing a thing, as for neglecting to know it. He would ask a boy a question, and if he did not answer it, he would beat him, without considering whether he had an opportunity of knowing how to answer it. For instance, he would call up a boy and ask him Latin for a candlestick, which the boy could not expect to be asked. Now, sir, if a boy could answer every question, there would be no need of a master to teach him." As a matter of fact, he said later of the same man : " My master whipt me very well. Without that, sir, I should have done nothing."

When he was fifteen he went to Stourbridge, and comparing his progress at the two schools in after years, he said : " At one, I learned much in the school, but little from the master : in the other, I learned much from the master, but little in the school." After he came down from Oxford he was forced, owing to his extreme penury, to accept a post as usher at Market Bosworth School, an employment he exceedingly disliked and complained of as being as " unvaried as the note of the cuckoo " ; that he did not know whether it was more disagreeable for him to teach, or the boys to learn, the grammar rules. He married soon afterwards and started a private academy at Edial, near Lichfield. Of his three pupils David Garrick was one. This was given up after eighteen months.

It is, in passing, very strange to notice how many of the world's geniuses have come up against the world of school.

The necessary routine and rigid command to "Conform or Go" of the public school system has crushed the spirits of so many that might have been great poets or painters if they had been encouraged to develop their imaginative faculties rather than to repress them, that we cannot help feeling grateful to the great men who have rebelled, as Johnson did, and given to the world what was in danger of being lost in a school.

Charles Lamb has two essays in which he devotes his critical humour to a picture of schoolmasters. The first, "Five and Thirty Years Ago," deals with his own masters at Christ's Hospital when he was a boy.

"Under the Rev. Matthew Field we lived a life as careless as birds. We talked and did just what we pleased, and nobody molested us. We carried an accidence for form: there was now and then the formality of saying a lesson, but if you had not learned it, a brush across the shoulders was the sole remonstrance. He came among us now and then, but often staid away whole days; and when he came, it made no difference to us—he had his private room to retire to, to be out of the sound of our noise.

" Boyer was a rabid pedant. His English style was crampt to barbarisms. He had two wigs, both pedantic, but of different omen. The one, serene, smiling, fresh powdered, betokening a mild day. The other, an old discoloured, unkempt, angry caxon, denoting frequent and bloody excursion.

Nothing was more common than to see him make a headlong entry from his inner recess, and with turbulent eye, singling out a lad, roar out, ' Od's my life, sirrah, I have a great mind to whip you,' then, with as sudden a retracting impulse, fling back into his lair—and after a cooling lapse of some minutes drive headlong out again with the expletory yell—' and I WILL, too!' "

The other essay of his on the subject is " The Old and the New Schoolmaster," in which he portrays the importunate questioning of the pedagogue on the coach between Bishopsgate and Shacklewell, the man full of information on every subject except those of real interest.

" Had he asked of me what song the sirens sang, or what name Achilles assumed when he hid himself among women, I might, with Sir Thomas Browne, have hazarded a ' wide solution.'

Rest to the souls of those fine old pedagogues, who, believing that all learning was contained in the languages which they taught, and despising every other acquirement as superficial and useless, came to their task as to a sport!

Revolving in a perpetual cycle of declensions, conjugations, syntaxes, and prosodies, life must have slipped from them at last like one day. The fine dream is fading away fast. The modern schoolmaster is expected to know a little of everything, because his pupil is required not to be entirely ignorant of anything. He must be superficially omniscient.

The least part of what is expected from him is to be done in school hours. He must seize every occasion—the season of the year—the time of the day—a passing cloud—a rainbow—a waggon of hay—a regiment of soldiers going by—to inculcate something useful. He must interpret beauty into the picturesque. A boy is at his board, and in his path, and in all his movements. He is boy-rid, sick of perpetual boy.

Why are we never quite at our ease in the presence of a schoolmaster? Because we know that he is not quite at his ease in ours. He is awkward, and out of place, in the society of his equals. He comes like Gulliver from among his little people, and he cannot fit the stature of his understanding to yours. He is so used to teaching that he wants to be teaching *you*. He can no more let his intellect loose in society than the clergyman can his inclinations. He is forlorn among his coevals: his juniors cannot be his friends."

Can any unprejudiced reader seriously aver

that "Elia" is unfair in his estimate of the profession? Is there not more than a little of truth in all that he has to say about them? Unfortunate perhaps it may be, but the deficiencies (and there must be some in every calling) are not accentuated or aggravated: of all writers Lamb may be taken as the fairest critic of a sadly misjudged race in the world of books.

I come now straight to the men of our own day who have specialised in giving us the master's point of view and idiosyncrasies rather than, as in the case of *Tom Brown's Schooldays*, portray boy's life at school alone.

I propose to omit the whole nineteenth-century school of writers from *Eric* to *Stalky*. They are too well known already, and are all romantically impossible and hopelessly out of date.

Rather would I push on to the first of the younger school of present-day writers headed by Mr. Walpole, who, for the first time in the history of the school story, drew pictures of the master's point of view rather than the boy's.

In *Mr. Perrin and Mr. Traill*, one of the most terrible books published in the twentieth century, Mr. Hugh Walpole has presented once and for all, as lightning flashes across our path, showing a yawning chasm at our feet where before we had in our blindness thought all safe, the hideous pettiness and ghastly ruin of soul and imagination and individuality that overtake the schoolmaster who gets into the rut, losing ambition, faith, hope, and charity. Were it not that I myself have had to live the very life depicted in this most magically real of books, I should probably join the great band of my profession who affect, albeit nervously, to scorn the types here drawn. "Of course there may be such schools as Moffatt's, but, thank God, this is not like it," say they, whereas they know in their heart of hearts that there is an almost uncanny reality about the conversations, the Common Room, the boys, and the whole deadening atmosphere; only those who have suffered so long as to be almost "soul-proof" can deny with any satisfaction the truth of Mr. Walpole's indictment.

We are first introduced to Mr. Perrin (who, I may as well confess now, happens to be a friend of mine) making good resolutions for the new term.

"'It *shall* be all right this term,' said Mr. Perrin. He was long and gaunt; his face might have been considered strong had it not been for a weak chin and a shaggy, unkempt moustache. His hands were long and bony, his eyes pale and watery, his age forty-five, and for twenty years he had been a master at Moffatt's."

The other chief actor in the drama, Traill, is described as "some one very young and very eager to make friends. His hair, parted in the middle and brushed back, was very light brown; his eyes were brown and his cheeks tanned. His figure was square, his back very broad, his legs rather short—he looked, beyond everything else, tremendously clean. He had learnt at Cambridge, above all things, one must not worry. His stay at Moffatt's was in the nature of an interlude: in a term or two he hoped to return to his old school, Clifton."

Of the others we glean a little at the masters' meeting.

The Rev. Moy-Thompson, the headmaster—a venerable looking clergyman—sat at the end of the table in an impatient way, as though he were longing for an excuse to fly into a temper. There was a tough stout man, by name Comber, once a famous football player, now engaged on a book on Athletics in Greece, a man with a heavy moustache and a sharp voice like a creaking door; a thin, bony little man with a wiry moustache and a biting cynical speech that seemed to goad Moy-Thompson to fury. There are others drawn to type, not worth mentioning, but this last man, Birkland by name (as Mr. Bradby would say, there is a Birkland in every school), is worth special mention because of a conversation he holds with young Traill which gives one the gist of Mr. Walpole's thesis. "Suddenly one evening Birkland asked him to come and see him. His room was untidy—littered with school books, exercise books, stacks of paper to be corrected; but behind this curtain of discomfort there were signs of other earlier things, some etchings, dusty and uncared for sets of Meredith and Pater, and a large engraving of Whistler's portrait of his mother."

Birkland starts the conversation by warning Traill to fly before the place seizes him, before it is too late.

"There are thousands of these places all over the country—places where the men are underpaid, with no prospects, herded together, all of them hating each other, wanting, perhaps, towards the end of term, to cut each other's throats. Do you suppose that that is good for the boys they teach? Get out of it, Traill, you fool! You say, in a year's time. Don't I know that? Do you suppose that I meant to stay here for ever when I came? But one postpones moving. Another term will be better, or you try for a thing, fail, and get discouraged, and then suddenly you are too old — too old at thirty-three — earning £200 a year — too old! and liable to be turned out if the Head doesn't like you.

"You must not be friends with the boys, because then we shall hate you and they will despise you. You will be quite alone. You think you are going to teach with freshness and interest—you are full of eager plans, new ideas. Every plan, every idea, will be killed immediately. It is murder—self-murder. You are going to kill every fine thought, every hope that you possess. You will never go anywhere because you are neglecting your work. You have no time. The holidays come, you go out into the world to find you are different from all other men. You are patronising, narrow, egotistic. Then marriage — no money, no prospects, starvation! And gradually there creeps over you a dreadful inertia—you do not care, you are a ghost."

So much for Birkland. As I said, there are Birklands in every school, and under their bitter irony there runs a vein of truth.

To return for a moment to Mr. Perrin: his conversation is so like that of all other schoolmasters in fiction that for the sake of coincidence I must quote one characteristic speech.

"I am afraid, friend Garden," he said, "that it will devolve upon your lordship—hum-ha—that you should write this poem of the noble Mr. Robert Browning's no less than fifty times. I grieve—I sympathise—I am your humble servant; but the law commands."

Do all of us, schoolmasters, talk like that? Writers seem to think we do, for they all unite to put conversations in our mouths of a most stilted, sarcastic, pedantic, unreal kind that I for one have never heard used at all by any member of any profession. I can quote no more, partly because of the horror and depression that grow on me as I read on, which I would not willingly bestow on any other human being, partly because I am convinced of the truth of so much of what Mr. Walpole says that it would be unfair to him to bring his thesis (which is a very serious one) down into line with all the rest of my authors. They never forget that their art is to please and consequently are driven to draw types, far removed in the main from the actual, of a kind calculated to make their readers laugh at the follies and pompous childishness of schoolmasters. Mr. Walpole has no time for laughter. He is far too serious for that.

But the book which above all others has fluttered the dovecots of the scholastic profession of late has been *The Lanchester Tradition*, by the Rugby housemaster, Mr. G. F. Bradby, who had already achieved a most enviable reputation as the author of *When every Tree was Green*, and *Dick*. This book is a veritable mine for our purpose, so much so that I must confine myself to a few of the more important points, hoping that every one interested in the subject will buy the book for himself and see the most powerful descriptions of public school masters in our language. The story, to put it shortly, shows how a certain school called Chiltern fared under the *régime* of a headmaster (Mr. Flaggon) of liberal opinions, and treats of his conflicts with his assistant masters, notably one Chowdler, the strong man of Chiltern.

"Mr. Chowdler owed his reputation for strength, not to any breadth of view or depth of sympathetic insight, but to a sublime unconsciousness of his own limitations. Narrow but concentrated, with an aggressive will and a brusque intolerance of all who differed from him, he was a fighter who loved fighting for its own sake and who triumphed through the sheer exhaustion of his enemies.

"A tall man, with broad shoulders, round bullet head, thin sandy hair, and full lips, he caught the eye in whatever company he might be.

"Mr. Flaggon had come to Chiltern with a determination to do great things for education. He himself had had a hard struggle to win to knowledge, and the phases of the struggle had left their mark deeply imprinted on his character. Born with a thirst for knowledge he had had to force his way to the fountain-head, and the narrow circumstances of a Cumberland vicarage had strewn the path with difficulties.

"Rather below middle height, with a clear-cut face and an intellectual forehead, his most striking feature was his eyes—fearless, grey, receptive eyes, which looked out on the world with a quiet but penetrating interest.

"Of public schools he knew nothing from the inside; *he had yet to learn how paralysing to the intellectual life an assured future may be.* In a word, he did not yet understand the psychology of the horse who refuses to drink when taken to the water; he knew what education ought to be, but he had not yet become acquainted with that particular breed of sheep that is born without an appetite. But as he mounted the Chiltern pulpit to deliver his first sermon from the text, 'The letter killeth, but the spirit maketh alive,' he felt conscious that here were no hungry sheep looking up to be fed, but indifference, inertia, and an unknown something that was probably worse than either and possibly the cause of both." To this sermon Mr. Chowdler, who was, of course, in orders, replied. "No mere layman could have combined such a capacity for quarrelling with so profound a conviction of his own reasonableness and humility."

The next master on the staff worthy of comment is Mr. Tipham, successor to a Mr. Cox who had resigned on the arrival of Mr. Flaggon.

" Mr. Tipham brought with him from Cleopas College, Cambridge, two more or less fixed ideas: first, that art consists in depicting disagreeable things in a disagreeable way, and secondly, that life in the twentieth century is governed by two conflicting forces—convention, which is always wrong, and nature, which is always right. This theory had carried him not only safely but brilliantly through his University career. He had secured a first in both parts of the Tripos; he had played a prominent part in the life of his own college and been quoted outside it. He had worn strange clothes, founded a literary society, and he had invented a new savoury. His slightly tilted nose and full cheeks gave him an air of confidence sometimes mistaken for conceit, while the long brown hair, drawn back over the temples and plastered down with fragrant oils, the orange tie and loose green jacket, proclaimed that he was one of those for whom art is not merely a hobby but an integral part of life. He smoked as he walked down to school from his lodgings and refused even a perfunctory homage to age and seniority. It was, indeed, soon evident that if the serious purpose of his life was to teach boys, his recreation consisted of shocking the masters. He went by the name of the 'Super-

Tramp' among the boys. Needless to say, his stay was brief" To return to Mr. Chowdler.

" When Mr. Chowdler's house was competing for laurels, Mr. Chowdler himself walked excitedly up and down the touch-line with a flushed face and protruding eyes, shouting instructions, such as, 'Pass, Percy, pass! Feet, feet, Gerald! Shoot, Basil, shoot, can't you? Stick to it! Good lads, all! Well *played*, Harry! well played, sir!" As a coach he had his limitations. For he had been brought up on the Rugby game, and was never accepted as an authority on the Chiltern game. Consequently his instructions were invariably ignored, but he continued to shout them in perfect good faith, and they were regarded as an inevitable, if irrelevant feature of the game."

By far the most amusing character on the staff is Mr. Bent the cynic (every staff, says the author, possesses a cynic).

He first comes into prominence at a bachelor dinner-party held in honour of Mr. Tipham, who arrived ten minutes late, clad in his usual outlandish garb, "rather like a man who has snatched up some clothes hurriedly to run to the bathroom, than a guest at a dinner-party."

Most of the party had been discomfited by this young man's preciosity.

" Mr. Bent had so far held himself in reserve, profoundly annoyed yet watching with a certain cynical enjoyment the growing irritation of his colleagues. But when, shortly after, Mr. Tipham laid it down as an axiom that *Dorian*

Grey was the greatest work of art that the human intellect has ever produced, he saw his opportunity and began in his best ironic vein:

"It's refreshing to hear you say that; so few people ever venture nowadays to express old-fashioned opinions, and the Victorians seldom get justice done to them by the rising generation. I am delighted to claim you as a Victorian." Tipham was violently annoyed at this, and raised his eyebrows and said coldly, "How so?" "If one wants to be in the swim nowadays," Bent continued, "one has to go into ecstasies over de Barsac or Roger Filkison. You read Roger Filkison, of course?"

Mr. Tipham admitted, with some reluctance, that he did not.

"Oh, he's the man, you know," replied Bent, "who writes the testimonials for the liver and kidney pills—the neo-realism they call it: very clever and morbid."

Later Mr. Tipham unbent over the post-impressionists and the masterly way in which Grummer painted flesh with one stroke of a glue-brush.

"I don't count him among the greatest masters," said Mr. Bent, "because he can't paint pimples." Again, later, in an argument on education with his friend Plummer, Mr. Bent remarks: "Knowledge only begins where middle-classdom ends. The art of being middle class consists in shutting yourself up in a detached house and only recognising the people who come in at the front door. Knowledge leads to the back door and the streets, and is therefore fatal to the art ; and knowledge is the goal of education ! . . . The English middle classes never have believed in education. The Scotch did once, till they discovered the superior merits of football."

His remarks are always pertinent and valuable. Here is one à propos of Chowdler :

" What *does* amaze me is that, with all his experience, Chowdler has never learned that boys encourage us in our illusions by quoting at us our own pet ideas and phrases. "

Or again, talking of the value of experience : " Pooh ! experience, indeed ; what's experience ? a snare and a delusion, unless you can bring an unbiased mind to bear on it, which schoolmasters never can. The man who looks at this view, for the first time, with the naked eye, sees far more of it than the man who looks at it for the hundredth time through smoked glasses. Experience is the smoke on the glasses ; it's the curse of our profession. We are all much more efficient when we're young than we ever are afterwards."

On the occasion of a house match · " To an observer of human nature," Mr. Bent explained, " nothing is so illuminating as the behaviour of a housemaster when his house is playing a match. Chowdler, of course, is elemental, and offers few points of interest ; he has the naked simplicity of the savage or the sportsman—blatant in victory, ungenerous in defeat. But Trimble is more complex and therefore more worthy of study. If I join him, he will affect an air of complete detachment and ask me for my views on Welsh Disestablishment or Woman Suffrage; but he will interrupt himself at intervals to murmur, 'Fools! asses! idiots! They deserve to be beaten!'"

"Chowdler being beaten," he continues later, "is a much more amusing spectacle than Chowdler winning. But I don't regard it as possible. He always keeps a reserve force—a kind of territorial army—of lean and hungry veterans with Christian names who have grown old in the service of their country. I am credibly informed that his senior fag, whom I see in the field, is a widower and maintains a family of four at Brighton. They all belong to the class which Chowdler designates as 'poor old' or 'good old,' and against this combination of age, godliness, and thrift, no ordinary house Eleven stands a chance."

This conversation occurred immediately before a most strenuous house match which Chowdler's house just managed to win after a titanic struggle. "Mr. Chowdler was swept away by a wave of intense, almost religious emotion. Foul play, monstrous decisions, past and present wrongs, were all forgotten for the moment. If the headmaster had come up and grasped him by the hand, he would have fallen upon the headmaster's neck—he would have fallen upon anybody's neck. Never since the relief of Ladysmith, where his own son was beleaguered, had he experienced such a sense of thankfulness, joy, and exultation. Perhaps it was an unconscious association of ideas which made him say to Mr. Tipham as he passed him: 'Thank God! We have kept the flag flying.' 'Where?' asked Mr. Tipham icily."

The result of this remarkable book has been that in every school where *The Lanchester Tradition* has been read the types represented by Chowdler, Bent, Flaggon, and Tipham have not only been recognised, but a universal vote would seem to show that here at any rate is no caricature. These four men really "live and move and have their being."

Now I have done, and I hope you find it a pleasant interlude. Surely in my own criticisms I have not been so wrong when by haphazard selection among great writers of every age I find every one to agree with my point of view.

However that may be, I can only press on in the hope that my fictional gallery has helped to impress on you the necessity for a change from a *régime* that permits of such teachers and such schools.

CHAPTER XVII

COMMON ROOM

THERE are many variations of Masters' Common Rooms, but the two main types may be roughly divided into those which are used as a club where masters meet and feed twice or thrice daily, — that is to say, Common Rooms in which men live almost entirely and are thrown upon the society of each other at every spare moment of the day,—and those Common Rooms where masters go, just by chance, for a smoke, to read the papers, and to find if possible a friend when they feel lonely.

It follows at once that the latter is the rarer but infinitely finer of the two; we will therefore leave it to the last. Schools conducted on the hostel system, where feminine influence is tabu, naturally economise by compelling their staffs to have their meals together.

Now breakfast of all meals is the one which the normal man prefers to eat alone, in peace, with the companionship only of his morning paper.

To share his habitual early morning "grumpiness" with thirty other irritable spirits, twenty-five of whom are thoroughly peevish because they cannot get at the papers which the five lucky ones do not appear to be reading, only serves to make a man really upset with life. He is ready to complain about everything: the weather, his food, his correspondence or the lack of it, the silly prattle of his neighbours, everything. I do not know anywhere which compares with a public school Common Room at breakfast for sheer downright rudeness and lack of courtesy.

After breakfast, irritability breaks out almost into feuds between cliques; a quite junior man will have taken most of the fire, and a ton of heavy asides about upstarts will be levelled at him by his seniors until he has the decency to go off to his rooms to correct work.

At the end of a hard day all the masters meet again for dinner. You might think that the cares of the day being over, a genial spirit of camaraderie would pervade the room. Not a bit of it. Rare indeed are those evenings when some luckless wight is not being hauled over the coals for omitting to tell a housemaster that he had caned So-and-so, had forgotten to punish So-and-so, had been seen smoking too near the school, had invited a certain boy too often to tea, had vented his wrath on the head of some poor innocent whose only fault was that he worked too hard.

Quarrels are only lightly disguised in these rooms. I have known two masters sit next to each other for two months, at two meals daily, and not interchange one syllable of conversation

—for all the world as if they were two sulky schoolgirls in the nursery.

There are many things that cause chafing among the very susceptible members of an average school staff. No drink, for instance, is ever allowed at Henstridge, only the senior vice-master has the privilege of imbibing seltzer-water for his health; no smoking except the cheapest of cheap cigarettes provided by the Common Room steward at a profit out of all proportion to their worth.

The atmosphere by the eighth or ninth week of term is charged with electricity: I have often wondered when two pugilistic-minded members of our fraternity would come to blows; and very near it do we get before the end of any term.

I would not dwell long upon such a Common Room: it is altogether evil; but it does exist.

At the other end of the scale we get the Common Room which really serves a useful purpose; it is the more ordinary type and exists in schools where most of the staff are married and are scattered about the town. It becomes then a real pleasure to have some meeting-place where we may discuss the match of yesterday, the plans for to-morrow's field day, or in a friendly manner quarrel over the absurd line taken by our acquaintance's favourite daily journal.

There are moments, of course, when such a room is to be avoided; at those "breaks" in the day's work when there is not time to go home, but there is time for a smoke and conversation:

then thirty men crowd and jostle one another in a room built to hold four or six comfortably

Of course to a journalist in search of copy any Common Room is a godsend, for there he will hear scraps of conversation which will provide him with valuable matter for his next school story.

He will hear why young Jenkins has never been caned, although he has deserved it daily for terms; he will hear repeated all those heavy sarcasms which Donaldson daily inflicts on his form; he will hear all the reasons why various victories and defeats have not been made public; he will hear healthy abuse of Williams by de Vincey, while Williams is out of the room, and equally violent abuse of de Vincey by Williams, while de Vincey is out of the room. He will hear all the local gossip, and a moment after the origin of phrases like "Hobson s choice," and "It's all my eye and Betty Martin"; he will hear learned disquisitions scattered with much classical quotation on Architecture, Home Rule, Serbia, Lord Northcliffe, Women, the O.T.C., Physical Drill, Geometry, and Aircraft.

But perhaps our young and keen new master will think that in the Common Room he will find, in the absence of his elders, much fine literary fare: he will be sadly disappointed.

The Spectator, *Blackwood's Magazine*, *Land and Water*, and *The Nineteenth Century* about exhaust the stock of periodicals to which a normal Common Room runs.

Few indeed allow the Liberal papers a hearing.

The Nation, The Saturday Review, Cornhill, The Fortnightly, the lighter weeklies, all the periodicals that you see in any mess are absent just where you would most naturally expect them; for if a schoolmaster is not liberal-minded, an omnivorous reader, how can you expect him to teach liberal-mindedness and a broad view of life?

A Common Room ought to be stocked with every variety of paper, magazine, and book. It ought to be a complete reference library. It ought to be a place where a man can procure every sort of smoke and drink, both of which make for good comradeship. It ought to be upholstered and kept like a good London club, a place where you can dine and give dinners, if you wish it, to any friends.

It ought to be a place over the portal of which should be written: "All shop abandon ye who enter here."

No petty school scandal or querulous complaint about the routine ought to be so much as mentioned: men should cast their gowns in the vestibule, and enter as free men of the world, citizens where all school degrees should be forgotten: just friends anxious to throw off the burden of the day, so that in each other's society they may find matter for recuperation in themselves. A glorious vision, but, oh! how sadly far away and impossible! Until schoolmasters are paid a minimum wage of £1000 a year such things can hardly be. So again do we see the power of wealth.

CHAPTER XVIII

A MASTERS' MEETING

MASTERS' meetings vary very much in kind and in degree.

They depend vastly upon two things: the type of headmaster who presides over them, and the time of the term in which they are held.

With regard to the latter first.

The first meeting of a school term, usually held on the day before the boys come back, is almost hilarious; every man is genuinely pleased to be back at his work, genuinely glad to meet his fellow-craftsmen. All are healthy, free of care, bronzed, full of anecdotes of Scotland, work with the Army or Red Cross, accidents by flood or field, record climbs, wonderful walks or motor tours, quaint friendships which they made, mutual acquaintances with whom they came into contact.

It is with difficulty that they can be got to bring their minds down to the schedule and change of routine which is about to be proposed.

The meeting starts quietly enough with little or no discussion about points that usually arise, but are considered as trifling, petty.

The scheme of work for the term is read out, and each man tots up his spare hours to see if he is being let off more or less work than he is accustomed to. Whisperings are heard between friends. "Oh, Heavens! what's the use of being out between 10.15 and 10.45? What I want is an extra half. Old Dodson has two extras a week: he can get away practically whenever he likes."

"I do like a chance of a good bath and a sound tea after Corps Parade, and now I'm switched on to modern shell French at 4.15 on Tuesdays: curse it."

Subdued murmurs of this nature keep us all occupied until a startling change is read out:

"In future no boy may go to the following shops without leave."

Half the staff is up in arms at once. One housemaster declares that his boys have dealt at such and such a shop, now tabu, for over one hundred years; another points out that Spofforth's is the only tailor within reach of his house; he is peculiarly averse from allowing his boys into the south end of the town—and so on. For half an hour the debate rages: solely between housemasters, for it is housemasters alone who are concerned. That is the way with most masters' meetings.

They are held at a time which causes the younger men to curtail their holiday quite needlessly by twenty-four hours, for there is never anything mooted which so concerns them that it could not all be written down on a sheet of memorandum paper and delivered to them on the first day of term.

Hours of precious time are spent in a discussion as to whether cricket shall precede choir practice, or choir practice cricket; music-master and games manager have a wordy battle which threatens to last through the night; meanwhile the rest, oblivious of the point at issue, or caring nothing for it, settle down to a book, if they have had the good sense to bring one in, or to drawing caricatures of their neighbours, if they are bookless.

I suppose, in fact I know, that many boys think these meetings to be wonderful affairs in which matters of state, of the greatest secrecy, are openly divulged and discussed.

I say that I know this, for what else could have induced that sportsman of long ago, Martin mi, whose valiant death at Hooge we all mourned only so little a time ago, to have concealed himself under the table during one of these meetings and courted the severe flogging which such an exploit was most certainly not worth? Incidentally, though the boy heard no secrets, and never would, however many such meetings he clandestinely attended, he did receive his thrashing, for he had the misfortune to hit on a day when the headmaster chose to remain behind after the meeting was over for three hours working over a knotty point in a revised scheme. The boy, driven to despair, could stand it no longer after 10 p.m., and crawled ignominiously from his hiding-place and stood, waiting for judgment, before his chief.

It is said, too, that clusters of boys used to rush into the room as soon as it was vacated on the off chance of seeing some damning piece of evidence written down and carelessly left behind. Their astonishment must have been great when they found no incriminating documents, but only little crumpled pieces of paper with—

"You swine! where's your Common Room sub?"

"What about that bottle of whisky?"

"Can you poss. dine—the usual time?"

"Aren't you fed up with this? Chicky's in for the night," scribbled on them, varied by gross libels on the facial disfigurements of most of the masters by such as could or could not draw.

But nowadays the school custos sweeps away every piece of paper immediately after a meeting, so that no trace of the mysterious talk, no vulgar caricature of the chaplain or art master may be treasured up by souvenir-seeking youth.

As a matter of fact, boys always seem to know more of the internal government of the school than any except the housemasters.

There are those of us who think it rather pitiful, if not wantonly outrageous, that we are kept in the dark about some great catastrophe which has overtaken the community for which we, in our small way, are just as responsible as the housemasters; and sometimes when we feel that the atmosphere is heavily charged and that there is a big row impending we wonder when first we shall be officially told.

As a matter of fact, we are never told, and as a consequence give ourselves away hopelessly in form for weeks after through pure ignorance. No—like most meetings of Secret Societies, masters' meetings accomplish very little.

Except at the beginning of term they are as often simply an occasion for the display of ill-feeling: every man has his own axe to grind, his own boys to push forward, his own *bête noire* to crush; and for my part I would abolish all meetings between the eighth and last week of term, because the nerves of most of us by that time are so shattered that we say more than we mean in our eagerness to have our own way and to dethrone an adversary.

The last meeting of term is, of course, necessary, but even then most men are already clad in holiday garb, an unconscious symbol that they are already in mind far away from the school, and their hearts are not altogether in the matters under discussion.

This time, if a boy came in and gathered up the fragments of notes, he would probably gather the impression that Bradshaw was the major topic of discussion.

But as I said at the beginning, as well as the time and the place, it is the headmaster that alters the character of these meetings.

The autocratic tyrant who convenes a meeting solely for the sake of hearing his own voice, and throws out suggestions, meaning them to become laws in any case, can scarcely be said to be doing the school much good by calling together his staff to hear new rules that he might just as well have printed and circulated without talking about them.

Such a man only invites covert animosity by saying, " Gentlemen, I propose to change the school game from Soccer to Rugger : I should like to hear your views " Follows, somewhat naturally, an almost panic-stricken howl with one accord from nearly every one. He listens patiently for half an hour and then cuts in with—

" Thank you, gentlemen ; I have been much interested. I cannot say that you have convinced me that I am wrong ; but I am glad to have heard your point of view : none the less we shall play Rugger as from the first day of next term. And now, gentlemen, to pass to the next point, I propose to bring in a new rule about boys going from one house to another or to masters' houses. I do not think any good is to be derived from too much communication of boys with one another (outside their own houses) or with masters. Masters will therefore see to it that in future no boy is entertained at their houses unless he happens to be a member of that house. I have several adequate reasons for this, but I should be glad to hear what my colleagues have to say."

His colleagues have to say a great deal, but he dismisses them, when he wishes to proceed, in a word, "Thank you, gentlemen; there is just one other point I wish to raise, the question of attendance in chapel . . ." So it goes on. To attend such a meeting is like being a courtier in the palace of a sultan, or that famous one in *Alice in Wonderland*: "Off with his head."

These strong, self-willed men have their uses: as the "boss" of a cotton combine, for instance, or as an unscrupulous newspaper proprietor such a man would be invaluable. As the headmaster of such a delicate organism as a public school he is worse than useless; he is comparable only to a child attempting to mend a valuable wrist-watch by twisting its works about with a rusty nail. Luckily this type is not common. The more normal headmaster really uses these meetings as gauges to see which way the wind blows; he collects his staff in order to ascertain their united or individual opinions on every branch of school life. The unfortunate part of the business is that such excellent gatherings should nearly always degenerate into quibbles between opponents with regard to some quite trivial by-product of school life, whereas by a little unselfishness, a little leaven of idealism, such meetings might be invaluable as showing the temper, aims, failures, and successes of the school.

Just as there is a distinctly felt, but quite unanalysable atmosphere in every school, quite different from every other; just as you can always distinguish an old Wykehamist from an old Harrovian almost as soon as you speak to him, so is there an indefinable something which characterises and yet differentiates every school staff. And this something is in nearly all cases very precious: it is consolidated and naturally most felt when the staff meet together. If they are tactfully handled by a sympathetic headmaster, all the best that is in each of them will come out at these meetings; each man will have something to say, some quota to contribute to the general welfare of the school. But there must be sympathy; there must be a full and adequate understanding between the different members; and, above all, youthfulness with its consequent bold experiments should not be crushed or discouraged, but shown gently how to tell its wheat from its tares.

There is always a danger in most masters' meetings of settling down into two rabid camps, age *versus* youth: the old men openly deriding the proposals of the young men; the young men covertly sneering at the antiquated, obsolete methods of the old.

If only a gentler spirit were encouraged so that the old would not think themselves too perfect to learn from the young, if only the young were not so sure of themselves that they pay no heed to the excellent side of the old, there might be a far finer system of education in vogue now than actually exists.

We hope (almost in vain) for a millennium when these meetings will be frequent and characterised by frankness and friendliness, when every sort of topic concerned with school life will be rationally discussed, and remedies and changes brought about with less rancour and desperate ill-feeling than at present obtains.

Either a masters' meeting is an occasion for full and free discussion or it is an unmitigated nuisance, an intolerable bore, an occasion for evil-speaking and evil-thinking at the worst, or placid contempt and aloofness, followed by practice in the art of the caricature, at its best. Either abolish them altogether if they concern two-thirds of the company not at all, or if they refuse to discuss the management of the school, or make them much more frequent and allow every man the right to suggest reforms or the abolition of some existent fungus.

CHAPTER XIX

END OF TERM

THE last weeks of term are very like the last three hundred yards of a three-mile race. All through the preceding months you have been strenuously trying to move at your fastest speed, and by the end of the twelfth week are so tired that you doubt whether you can last another lap, when suddenly you are faced with examinations and have to redouble your efforts. Papers that have to be refreshing and original, when you are dying of exhaustion and have no mind left, are not the joy to set that parents imagine. The blue-pencilling of errors that seem to crop up a millionfold more abundantly at the time of trial than ever they did in practice make you gnaw your moustache with rage, and certainly do not raise the laughter in you which they seem to cause among the readers of *Punch*. The constant sitting-in and invigilating are far more boring and deadly than teaching the most stupid of boys the most lifeless of subjects.

Night after night you are deprived of sleep by having to stay up till the small hours correcting hundreds of papers, and then, after one agelong week of such life, you have to collect all your results and make up orders that appear to you to be far from correct, and you have to report on the excellence (how rare !) and the failure (how extraordinarily frequent l) of each boy whom you have examined. The last day comes, and with it a final burst, almost with teeth and fists clenched and eyes shut in your frenzy to get everything done in time, and you find yourself, with hair touzled, temper lost, rings under your eyes, and cheeks hollow and sunken, on the platform in Big School listening to the parting words of advice from the headmaster to the assembled three hundred.

"It has been a better term than might have been expected; of course your corps work has been the predominant feature, and now don't imagine that you can relax your efforts in the holidays. The happiness of your coming free time is going to be the sort of happiness that comes from helping others; there is work for you to do, in the Y.M.C.A. army tents, or as advised by the Cavendish Association, about which I have just told you." The terminal concert follows, filled with khaki-clad old boys at the back, who have, by a miracle, all obtained leave to come back for a farewell visit before going out to the Front.

Stanford's rendering of "The Revenge" causes us to feel thrills of pride of country and of our naval history, thrills which become intensified as we listen to "The Death of Nelson," sung immediately afterwards by one who has just gained his commission and leaves us to-morrow ; all the National Anthems of the Allies and the school " Carmen " make the rafters ring again, and we all troop out to house suppers, informal gatherings of friendly cliques over a last meal ; none of the old formality, calling attention to this or that cup or colour won, this or that success gained. No, this term we just sit down anywhere, cheerfully " ragging " our nearest neighbours, and shout for songs or speeches as we feel like them . . . and so to bed, but not to sleep.

The boys from over-excitement, the thoughts of the liberty of the morrow, the masters from over-fatigue, toss and turn through the night but scarcely sleep.

As soon as dawn breaks, up rises the entire school, pillow-fights follow, friendly feuds, a last packing of trifles, a careless farewell, and 8.40 sees the school close deserted, forsaken, quiet.

In the streets in the morning may be seen stragglers who have been kept back for some breach of rules, mortified beyond expression, scowling at every passer-by, almost counting the minutes until the time of release. Master meets master aimlessly wandering about, and greets him with, " Good, isn't it, to have absolutely nothing to do for a day ? "

At two o'clock the main quadrangle is peopled again for the last time for four weeks with toga-ed figures hurrying with mark-books and suggestions to the Common Room for the masters' meeting. Faced with a clean piece of foolscap on which to write his thoughts, each man immediately begins to pencil out a ghastly sketch of his neighbour with fiendish delight, and then, as if proud of the result, to continue to repeat the operation a hundred times on every available space until the meeting is over.

Promotions are read out, prizes are awarded, notes of extreme urgency are passed from master to master; some hurriedly add up marks with feverish energy, others, frankly bored, yawn and close their eyes.

At last it is over. A buzz of conversation breaks out; names like Edinburgh, Devonport, Eastbourne, Tidworth, Buxton, take the place of marks. Every one is free, free for four whole weeks: free to smoke where he likes, free to wear what clothes he likes—this meeting is a revelation in sartorial taste: normally we are indistinguishable one from another—blue suits, black ties, dark shoes and socks make us all alike, but to-day is a kind of "coming of spring"; the lightest of light Norfolk coats, soft silk collars and garishly coloured ties, socks of delicate greys and browns, waistcoats even more daring, all these clash strangely with our sombre surroundings in this old oak room.

No more getting up at unearthly hours, nor hustling through meals in order to get to school in time; from being merely masters of others, for a brief space of time we are now permitted to be masters of ourselves. Strange, too, how the grey old courts change in a twinkling. This morning saw them full of myriad boys scuttling away for their trains; lunch-time saw them deserted as a disused mill; now we pour out of Common Room and hear the ringing laughter of children and girls. The masters' wives and daughters have usurped our sacred precincts for a game of hockey, and newly returned boys from far-away preparatory schools are showing how immeasurably superior they are now at the game to their elders or friends of old.

A short farewell for our colleagues, and we separate to the ends of the earth. No talk, however, this time of walking tours and Mediterranean voyages under the guidance of one Doctor Lunn; what all our conversation turns on is, "What regiment are you attached to? What? Good Lord! Tidworth for Easter? And take your own blankets! What a sweat! Oh! I'm going to the 9th East Lancs, Kitchener's, at Eastbourne. So long, old boy. Cheeroh!"

My train doesn't go for another hour; my house is shut up, everything put away, now bare and ugly. I cannot face it, so I take my bicycle and go up over West Hill for a last look at my favourite scenery.

As I go along I find myself living over again the petty trials and triumphs of the term. Yonder gap in the field was the scene of my capture on night operations in March. Oh, bitter moment! Those fields where the trees cluster together are where I outflanked old "Toothpick," who thinks his platoon inviolable. That plough to which we are just coming marks the end of a grand seventy-minute run with the Beagles, only two up at the death and they "dead to the world."

On this road how often in the dust, or the rain, or the wind have we marched gaily along as a corps! I can almost hear the "Carmen" now as we rend the air with our shouts. Oh! boys, boys, why will you make us love you so, and passing, forget? . . . "But no more of that, for that way sadness lies."

At the summit of the hill, panting, I stand on the top of a high hedge and survey the great, bare, rolling downs which stretch before me all over the south of Wessex, just beginning to revive again with the joyous birth of spring. What a country! How hard to leave you when the time comes! I have brought to you my sorrows and my joys, and always you have filled me with comfort. It seems ungrateful in me to leave you now. It was ever the same.

Anxious, pining for the holidays to come, when they arrive I find myself bored, irritable, restless, unwilling to go away. Hurriedly I turn my back, mount my bicycle, and descend into the valley.

The train comes in all too soon. Reluctantly I take my seat in it and settle back to think . . . and then a stranger starts to talk. Back to the war—back to the world—the school doors are shut; I am as if I had never been near school. Yet to-morrow at home the ache will be worse. These first few days of the holidays, they are terrible; the longing for those merry, careless voices, even for those worries and hours of overwork, all would be welcome contrasted with our life of aimless meanderings at home.

We write many letters to friends to keep us in touch with the life we have left, to every boy of whom we can think, to nearly all our colleagues ; and gradually Time, the only healer of wounds, causes the pain to be less severe, our longing to be less poignant—the holidays have begun.

Printed by MORRISON & GIBB LIMITED, *Edinburgh*

BSW 5M.915

CPSIA information can be obtained at www.ICGtesting.com
Printed in the USA
LVOW07s0310141115

462583LV00029B/791/P